European Budget and Sustainable Growth

The Role of a Carbon Tax

P.I.E. Peter Lang

Bruxelles · Bern · Berlin · New York · Oxford · Wien

Alberto Majocchi

European Budget and Sustainable Growth

The Role of a Carbon Tax

Federalism,
Vol. 10

This book was made possible by the Centro Studi sul Federalismo of Turin (www.csfederalismo.it)

This publication has been peer reviewed.

International Academic Publishers
Brussels, 2018
1 avenue Maurice, B-1050 Brussels, Belgium
brussels@peterlang.com; www.peterlang.com

Printed in Germany

ISSN 2294-6969
ISBN 978-2-8076-0985-3
ePDF 978-2-8076-0986-0
ePUB 978-2-8076-0987-7
MOBI 978-2-8076-0988-4
DOI 10.3726/b15016
D/2018/5678/102

Bibliographic information published by "Die Deutsche Nationalbibliothek".

"Die Deutsche National Bibliothek" lists this publication in the "Deutsche Nationalbibliografie"; detailed bibliographic data is available on the Internet at <http://dnb.de>.

Table of contents

Part I

Fiscal policy in the European Union

Part II

New resources for the EU budget

Part I

Fiscal policy in the European Union

Chapter 1

Introduction

In the current context of the European Union the idea of enlarging the size of the budget and financing this increase with additional own resources could seem largely unrealistic. But there are two points to bear in mind within this framework. The speech of French President Emmanuel Macron at the Sorbonne University[1] represents a radical change of approach to the European Union's political issues, stressing that the main problems that Europe is obliged to face cannot be solved at the national level. Furthermore, and this is the second remark, after a long period of austerity, and with the substantial support of an expansionary monetary policy by the European Central Bank, the European economy has recovered after a period of deep recession and now the trend of growth seems upwards. But, in the meantime, new urgent problems have emerged that require a European solution: worldwide competition is growing, the transition to the digital economy requires significant investment and the education of a highly-cultivated human capital, and climate change weighs seriously on the future of the human race. The problems of internal and external security seem even more urgent; these require steps forward in the field of foreign and security policy and a large amount of money to be invested supporting a new "global strategy",[2] while the difficult task of controlling migration should be managed in a spirit of solidarity with the poorest countries of the world.

It seems reasonable to recognise that all these challenges require an increased role for the European Union, especially in the area of defence and security policy, and for the Eurozone as well, if the risks of a new financial and economic crisis have to be managed with adequate means and if Europe wants to avoid another double-dip recession. Hence, in view of the difficult process of approval of the Multiannual Financial

1 *Initiative pour l'Europe*. Discours d'Emmanuel Macron: *Pour une Europe souveraine, unie, démocratique*, Paris, 26 Septembre 2017. The availability to increase the German contribution to the EU budget has been expressed clearly in the new German government's coalition agreement signed by the CDU and the SPD.

2 European Commission, *A Global Strategy for the European Union*, 19 June 2017.

Framework (MFF), the time seems ripe to begin an in-depth evaluation of the new resources that are needed to fund an enlarged EU budget, including a budget line specifically targeted at financing Eurozone needs – in particular through the setting up of a Stabilisation Fund dedicated to the euro area in order to guarantee the stability of the single currency.

There are many proposals on the table regarding the resources that can be used to finance the EU budget. The Commission has proposed[3] for the 2021-27 MFF a basket of new own resources, comprising: a) 20% of the revenues from the Emission Trading System; b) a 3% rate applied to the new Common Consolidated Corporate Tax Base; c) a national contribution calculated on the amount of non-recycled plastic packaging waste in each Member State (€0.80 per kilo). This portion of own resources is estimated to amount to an annual average of around €22 billion, corresponding to approximately 12% of the total revenues, finally permitting an increase in the size of the budget, if the political will to proceed along this path is there. This is the main point, since without new, additional resources, the Union will not be able to efficiently face the challenges with which Europe is currently confronted. The new receipts proposed by the Commission could be complemented by other resources flowing from a digital tax or by reforms to VAT.

From this perspective, a crucial role is played by putting a price on the use of carbon, that could guarantee the achievement of a double dividend. Together with other new resources, its receipts provide the possibility for a progressive increase in the size of the EU budget, in order to promote economic growth, to create a stabilisation fund, to support competitiveness of European production during the transition to a digital economy and, at the same time, to guarantee internal and external security. Moreover, the revenues flowing from carbon pricing could be used to largely fund an Energy and Environment Agency, derived from the expected revision of the Euratom Treaty. Therefore, putting a price on the consumption of fossil fuels emitting carbon dioxide could endow the Agency with the capacity to smooth the transition to a carbon-free economy, using the funds to promote investments in renewable energy sources and to provide training and additional skills for workers made redundant in declining sectors of the economy. Additionally, at the level of Member States part of the revenues could be employed in avoiding the regressive impact of energy taxation through a reduction of income tax rates on the most deprived families.

---

3 European Commission, *A modern budget for a Union that protects, empowers and defend*, Brussels, 2 May 2018.

Carbon pricing is thus a key to start up a new phase of sustainable growth of the European economy and to fund the investments needed for internal and external purposes. But it must be kept in mind that this is not a new tax, but a way "to get prices right", by including in the price of goods negative externalities deriving from the combustion of fossil fuels utilised in their production; this measure could be supported by public opinion, more and more concerned about the risks of an ecological holocaust.

The achievement of this objective is difficult since, according to existing rules, any decision in the fiscal area is constrained by the approval of 27 Member States.[4] Until such time that an effective federal Constitution is put in place, each government remains linked to its national political constituency; and the European Commission, that should guarantee that decisions are taken in pursuit of the European interest, is still politically too weak to comply with this task. A real reform of the budget to promote an effective European fiscal policy is conceivable only, as Monnet said, when Member States are involved in a deadlock where "…it is possible to come out only in a way: with a concrete and unwavering action on one point, limited, but crucial, that will bring about a radical change on this point and will modify progressively all the data of the problem…".[5] In this phase of the history of European unification, the financing of the budget with new own resources and, more specifically, with a carbon tax, seems to represent exactly the point that Monnet envisaged.

If Europe wants to safeguard its wellbeing and to play a significant role in international affairs, a national solution is no longer available and a step forward towards a federal Constitution appears to be urgently required.[6] The elections to the European Parliament in 2019 will oblige political forces to define a position on all the different topics with which Europe

---

4 Or less, if a smaller group of countries decides to proceed forward with a Permanent Structured Cooperation – Articles 42(6) and 46 TEU – towards an "ever closer Union among the peoples of Europe", as it was affirmed in the Preamble to the Rome Treaty.

5 "Il Memorandum Monnet del 3 maggio 1950", in M. Albertini, *Il federalismo. Antologia e definizioni*, Il Mulino, Bologna, 1979, p. 286.

6 "France and Germany share a common ambition for the European project: a democratic, sovereign and united Europe, a competitive Europe, a Europe that is a basis for prosperity and defends its economic and social model and cultural diversity, a Europe that promotes an open society, based on shared values of pluralism, solidarity and justice, upholding the rule of law everywhere in the EU and promoting it abroad, a Europe that is ready to assert its international role to promote peace, security and sustainable development and be a leader in the fight against climate change, a Europe that successfully address the migration challenge" (Meseberg Declaration, 19 June 2018, signed by Emmanuel Macron and Angela Merkel).

is confronted; public opinion should play its role as well. But it is important to be aware that the era of Monnet's *small steps* is finished forever. If Europe wants to survive, a big leap forward is unavoidable and the task of the political class is to promote a deeper understanding of the risks implicit in the current stalemate, while showing the advantages deriving from the creation of federal institutions that will provide Europe with a real and democratic decision capacity.

CHAPTER 2

Fiscal rules in the Monetary Union

1. The logic underlying the process towards the Maastricht Treaty

The project of an Economic and Monetary Union within Europe started as a necessary outcome of the completion of the Internal Market. Since the EMS had created a condition of relative monetary stability, it was possible to proceed to the elimination of the other barriers that prevented the Common Market being considered as an effective internal market. The Delors project, exploiting the new institutional rules included in the Single Act, included the idea of different stages in order to achieve the four fundamental freedoms foreseen by the Rome Treaty (free movement of goods, services, capital and persons), starting from January 1, 1993. But once the free movement of capitals had been guaranteed, monetary policy would become totally ineffective: during a recession, if a national Central Bank were to reduce interest rates in order to support the recovery, an outflow of domestic capital would follow, since the level of interest rates is higher abroad, and the opposite would happen if interest rates were raised to fight inflation, since capital inflows prevent the achievement of the deflationary goal. Hence, a process towards a single currency in order to regain, at the European level, the freedom of action lost at the national level appeared inevitable. This was the basis on which the Treaty approved in Maastricht on December 11, 1991, signed by Member States on February 7, 1992, was conceived.

The Treaty was based on two fundamental principles. The first decision was to proceed by stages towards the final goal of a Monetary Union. This method was quite different from the *shock therapy* adopted in the case of the German monetary unification. In this last case, political unification took place before the start of Monetary Union. Hence, the German federal government was able to control the process leading to the single German currency, with the possibility to use all the domestic instruments of economic policy – of fiscal and monetary nature. In the European case, monetary unification took place in a confederal framework, where the only instrument of economic policy was the coordination of national decisions. As such, Germany, the country that had to bear the largest costs in giving up monetary sovereignty, wanted to ensure that the convergence process, in terms of inflation, fiscal and monetary discipline, could be completed in time in order to avoid the risk of negative externalities deriving from incorrect behaviour of other countries.

The second decision – that followed from the method of gradualism adopted – was to establish right from the beginning the conditions that should be met to join the single currency. This choice was particularly significant as far as fiscal discipline is concerned. In the Treaty, the highest level of budgetary deficit was fixed at 3% and the highest level of public debt at 60%. This rule has been largely criticised since these numbers appeared arbitrary. The real reason underlying this choice was the fear that the principle of no-bail out included in the Treaty might proves inadequate, since Member States, if not constrained by rigid fiscal rules, could reach a point where the risk of default due to excessive debt levels would make a support intervention of the European Central Bank, as a lender of last resort, unavoidable – imperilling the financial stability of the Monetary Union.

2. Maastricht constraints and fiscal policy

In the Maastricht Treaty problems of public finance were considered in particular with reference to the definition of an excessive deficit. In fact, Article 126 TFEU[7] set the conditions which a country had to respect in order to join the Monetary Union, while the actual numbers were defined by the Protocol on the procedure for excessive deficits, which called for "3% for the ratio between the budget deficit, forecast and actual, and gross domestic product at market prices; 60% for the ratio between the public debt and GDP at market prices". It is clear that this aspect of the Treaty was particularly relevant and the political debate and the attention of public opinion focussed mainly on these conditions.

In fact, setting a value equal to 3% of GDP for the deficit can be justified by referring to the *golden rule* of public finance, on the basis of which current expenditure must be financed by current revenues, while

7 The Articles of the Maastricht Treaty are referred to in the text with the numbers of the "Consolidated Version of the Treaty on the Functioning of the European Union", after the approval of the Lisbon Treaty.

investment spending can be financed by debt. In fact, in the period from 1974 to 1991 public investment in Europe averaged 3%. In reality, this condition of the Maastricht Treaty reflected, on the one hand, a condition that was widespread in local finance systems, where debt – destined to finance investment spending – cannot normally exceed certain levels; on the other hand, it avoided the formation of excessive deficits without tying deficit financing, through bond issues, to the distinction – in large part ambiguous and distorting – between current expenditures and investment expenditures.

A 3% deficit is compatible with the stabilisation of the debt/GDP ratio – which represents an essential condition for avoiding an excessive deterioration of public finance conditions in countries taking part in the Monetary Union – at a level that likewise depends on the nominal growth rate of GDP. On the basis of this condition,[8] if the deficit is 3%, then in order to guarantee the stabilisation of the debt/GDP ratio at the forecast level of 60%, the nominal growth rate of GDP has only to reach 5%. It is no coincidence, in fact, that this was the growth rate reached in Germany during the 1980s. The Maastricht rules thus fitted in perfectly with the German situation; moreover, they permitted the indirect introduction of a constraint for the rate of inflation as well – which the Treaty only set with reference to the three most effective countries.

The implementation of this rule is thus strongly conditioned by the rate of inflation, which influences the result through the nominal growth rate of GDP. Thus, while within a Monetary Union inflation rates tend to converge, it is difficult to claim that a definition of the equilibrium level of debt which is tied to the future inflation rate is entirely appropriate. From a technical point of view this rule thus appears arbitrary. But, instead, it had a politically decisive role: on the one hand, it confirmed the European countries' strong will to avoid the formation of an excessive stock of debt, destined to weigh down future generations; but above all – and this is the important point – the rule in question represented a necessary condition for obtaining German consensus on the loss of monetary sovereignty.

While recognising the non-absolute value of the Maastricht constraints, it must be remembered that these were nevertheless subject to relatively elastic interpretation. In particular, Article 126(3) TFEU established that "if a Member State does not fulfil one of both of these criteria [regarding level of

---

8 The stabilisation condition of the debt/GDP ratio is well known in the economic literature: $d = x.b$, where d is the budget deficit as a share of GDP, b is the debt/GDP ratio, and x the nominal growth rate of GDP (De Grauwe, *The Economics of Monetary Integration*, Oxford University Press, 1997, p. 133).

deficit and stock of debt], the Commission shall prepare a report. The report of the Commission shall also take into account whether the government deficits exceed investment expenditure and take into account all other relevant factors, including the medium-term economic and budgetary position of the Member State". And Article 126(2a) specified, where the procedures for realising the mechanisms of multilateral surveillance are defined, that a deficit above 3% could be considered not to be excessive if the ratio "...has declined substantially and continuously and reached a level that comes close to the reference value..."; or, alternatively, "...the excess over the reference value is only exceptional and temporary and the ratio remains close to the reference value...". At the same time, a debt/GDP ratio above 60% would not be considered excessive if "...the ratio is sufficiently diminishing and approaching the reference value at a satisfactory pace..." (Article 126(2b)).

The point here is that the political decision at Maastricht was not to consider excessive the deficits of those countries that had taken substantial steps in the direction indicated by the Treaty and/or were not too far from the reference values. Once a country became a member of the Monetary Union, the respect of the rules of convergence within the mechanism of multilateral surveillance – in particular with regard to excessive deficits – would have to be assured by the Commission, which nevertheless had a rather limited sanctioning power. As a result, these dispositions have been further supplemented by the approval of a Stability and Growth Pact.

3. From Maastricht constraints to the Stability Pact

The political debate on the development of Monetary Union was largely affected by German pressure to extend the Maastricht constraints beyond the start of the Monetary Union. The point of departure of this debate was represented in a speech in the Bundestag on November 7, 1995 by the German Finance Minister Waigel, where a new *Stabilitätspakt für Europa* was proposed, establishing the principle that deficits could not exceed the limit of 3% during a negative cyclical downturn, while in normal times the limit of the deficit could not be higher than 1%. The German proposal was first evaluated by a Commission's Note,[9] while a more in-depth analysis was contained in a subsequent Note.[10]

9 European Commission, *Towards a stability pact*, Note to the Monetary Committee, Brussels, 10 January 1996.

10 European Commission, *A stability pact to ensure budgetary discipline*, Note to the Monetary Committee, Brussels, 18 March 1996.

This Note underlined that in the EMU monetary policy is managed at the European level and must aim, as a priority goal, at price stability. As a consequence, "…budgetary policy, that remains under the responsibility of national authorities, should play an important role in macro-economic stabilisation during the economic cycle and in the case of asymmetric shocks…". The Commission remarked that a certain degree of flexibility must be guaranteed to the national budgets to make stabilisers, functioning during the cycle, automatic and to allow discretionary fiscal measures in the case of country-specific shocks. Hence, the proposal put forward by the German government was considered weak, since it did not take into account that national budgets were constrained in various ways, according to each economic system's different degree of convergence and the varying demographic perspectives in different countries. Furthermore, the room for manoeuvre that must be accepted in national budgetary policy, to effectively face different phases of the economic cycle, changes from one country to another and, generally, should be larger for small countries. Finally, previously accumulated stock of debt should be considered in order to plan different paths to compliance with the constraints defined in the Maastricht Treaty.

The main conclusions of this Commission's Note were the following:

a) a certain degree of differentiation in national medium-term budgetary goals seems desirable from an economic viewpoint;
b) putting a single deficit objective equal to 1% of GDP – as it has been established in the proposal for a Stability Pact – appears as arbitrary and, for many countries, insufficient either for coping with cyclical disequilibria or to face the consequences of the population's ageing;
c) when a medium-term budgetary objective at the national level has been established lower than 3%, a further constraint on the ratio debt/GDP is unneeded.

But a radical change in the Commission's stance – and a further tightening in the direction of the German proposal – appeared in a later Note[11], that reached a conclusion that presaged the final version of the Stability Pact:

> to keep budget discipline during the Phase three of the EMU represents an essential condition to exploit all the benefits of the single currency. The refer-

[11] European Commission, *Ensuring budgetary discipline in stage three of Emu*, Note for the Monetary Committee, Brussels, 19 July 1996.

ence value of 3% of GDP for the deficit must be considered as the upper limit during normal times. The strategy must be based on a two stages approach to budgetary discipline and to the coordination of budgetary policies: medium-term budget objective near to zero or in surplus, that allows to remain under the floor of 3% in normal times and provides the possibility of a certain degree of differentiation between Member States; coordination of budgetary policies at the Union's level to guarantee a coherent scheme for the whole Union.

In this Note the way was opened to the final version of the Stability and Growth Pact (SGP).

4. The content of the Stability and Growth Pact

In its final version the Stability and Growth Pact was a Resolution of the European Council (Amsterdam, June 17, 1997) engaging Member States to avoid excessive budgetary deficits, to guarantee budgets close to balance or in surplus, and two Council Regulations: No. 1466/97 of July 7, 1997 on the strengthening of the surveillance of budgetary positions and the surveillance and coordination of economic policies, and No. 1467/97 of July 7, 1997 on speeding up and clarifying the implementation of the excessive deficit procedure.[12]

The first Regulation stated that each Member State, whose currency is the euro, should submit to the Council and the Commission a *Stability Programme*[13] in the framework of the multilateral surveillance mechanism. Such a programme had to include the following information:

a) the medium-term objective for a budgetary position of close to balance or in surplus and the adjustment path towards this objective for the general government surplus/deficit and the expected path of the general government debt ratio;
b) the main assumptions about expected economic developments and important economic variables which are relevant to the realisation of the stability programme such as government investment expenditures, real gross domestic product (GDP) growth, employment and inflation;

12 The legal basis of the Stability and Growth Pact are Article 121 and 126 TFEU, and Article 136 establishing that the Council could "...adopt measures specific in those Member States whose currency is the euro...".

13 The Member States whose currency is not the euro shall submit to the Council a *Convergence Programme*.

c) a description of budgetary and other economic policy measures being taken and/or proposed to achieve the objectives of the programme and, in the case of the main budgetary measures, an assessment of their quantitative effects on the budget;
d) an analysis of how changes in main economic assumptions would affect the budgetary and debt position.

The Council should, within the framework of multilateral surveillance, examine whether the medium-term budget objective in the stability programme provided for a safety margin to ensure the avoidance of an excessive deficit; whether the economic assumptions on which the programme were based are realistic and whether the measures being taken and/or proposed were sufficient to achieve the targeted adjustment path towards the medium-term budgetary objective.[14] Where the Council, in accordance with Article 121 TFEU, considered that the objectives and contents of a programme should be strengthened, the Council should invite the Member State concerned to adjust its programme.

The second Regulation set out the provisions to accelerate and clarify the excessive deficit procedure, having as its objective the deterrence of excessive general government deficits and, if they occur, to further their prompt correction. The excess of a government deficit over the reference value should be considered exceptional and temporary when resulting from an unusual event outside the control of the Member State concerned and which has a major impact on the financial position of the general government, or when resulting from a severe economic downturn. The Commission should, as a rule, consider an excess over the reference value resulting from a severe economic downturn to be exceptional only if there is an annual fall in real GDP of at least 2%. The Council, when deciding whether an excessive deficit exists, had to take into account in its overall assessment the remarks made by the Member State concerned, showing that an annual fall of real GDP of less than 2% was nevertheless exceptional in the light of further supporting evidence, in particular on the abruptness of the downturn or on the accumulated loss of output relative to past trends.

Whenever the Council decided to apply sanctions to a participating Member State, a non-interest-bearing deposit was, as a rule, required.

---

14 Member States should pursue "...an appropriate annual improvement of its cyclically-adjusted budget balance, net of one-offs and other temporary measures, required to meet its medium-term budgetary objective, with 0.5% of GDP as a benchmark..." (Council Regulation No. 1466/97 of 7 July 1997, Article 5).

When the excessive deficit resulted from non-compliance with the criterion relating to the government deficit ratio, the amount of the first deposit would comprise a fixed component equal to 0.2% of GDP, and a variable component equal to one tenth of the difference between the deficit as a percentage of GDP in the preceding year and the reference value of 3% of GDP. Any single deposit would not exceed the upper limit of 0.5% of GDP. A deposit should, as a rule, be converted by the Council into a fine if, two years after the decision to require the participating Member State concerned to make a deposit, in the view of the Council the excessive deficit had not been corrected. Deposits were to be lodged with the Commission. Interest on the deposits and the fines constituted other revenue referred to in Article 201 of the Treaty and should be distributed among Member States – whose currency is the euro – without an excessive deficit, in proportion to their share in the total GDP of the eligible Member States. It appeared politically inappropriate that countries that are not part of the euro area could also benefit from this mechanism.

5. From the SGP to the Fiscal Compact

The Stability and Growth Pact entered into force in 1997. In 2005 EU law makers amended the SGP to allow it to consider in more depth individual national circumstances and to add more economic rationales to the rules to be complied with. Surveillance and co-ordination were strengthened and the excessive deficit procedure was clarified and its implementation accelerated. In 2011 the SGP was made more comprehensive and predictable with a major enhancement of the EU's economic governance rules through a collection of new laws, known as the *Six Pack*. The monitoring of both budgetary and economic policies was organised under the European Semester and further details on the implementation of the SGP's rules were laid down in the Commission document on flexibility.[15]

Adherence to the SGP was further strengthened by new laws known as the *Two Pack*, which reinforced economic coordination between Member States and introduced new monitoring tools for the euro area. But the most important step forward in reinforcing the rules of the SGP was achieved in 2013 with the approval of the *Fiscal Compact* (FC), which was a part of an intergovernmental Treaty known as the Treaty on Stability, Coordination and Economic Governance. The budgetary targets set by

---

15 European Commission, *Making the best use of the flexibility within the existing rules of the stability and growth pact*, COM(2015) 012 final, Brussels, 10 February 2015.

the SGP's preventive arm (the Medium-Term Objectives) were newly defined, stating that the structural deficit – net of the cycle's influence – should not be higher than 0.5%, while the gap between the current ratio of the stock of debt to GDP and the floor of 60% should be reduced by 5% each year. Control procedures and sanctions were foreseen in the FC to prevent non-compliance with the rules.

This was a very strongly strengthened budgetary rule, since a budget close to balance or in surplus must also include investment expenditure. In the classical theory of public finance, the most accepted version of the *golden rule*[16] implies that current expenditures must be covered by fiscal receipts, but that investments could be financed either through current account surpluses or by issuing public bonds (with some limits, fixing for instance the maximum amount of tax revenues that could be appointed to cover the interest expenditures tagged to servicing the stock of debt).

This classic version of the *golden rule*[17] is justified by the fact that an expenditure, whose effects are extended for a long period of time – in some cases for many decades – could not be covered in a single year and should be spread through a series of following budgets. Furthermore, if public investments promoted higher growth, new revenues would be provided in the budget, favouring the coverage of investment costs.

The hypothesis underlying the rule of a budget close to balance is the Ricardian equivalence, where savers are supposed to be wholly rational and perfectly informed, so that a current deficit implies that taxes must be increased in the future to cover the service of the debt. Hence, saving must be raised to face future costs and, consequently, domestic demand shrinks. On the contrary, if the budget is close to balance, or in surplus, savers' and domestic and international investors' expectations change, interest rates diminish with positive effects on the budget due to the lower costs of servicing the debt. As a consequence, more resources could be devoted to fund public investments with an ensuing increase in the rate of growth of the economy.

---

16 R.A. Musgrave, "The nature of Budgetary Balance and the Case for a Capital Budget", in *American Economic Review*, 1939, pp. 260-271; R.A. Musgrave, *The Theory of Public Finance. A Study in Public Economy*, New York, McGraw-Hill, 1959.

17 "The SGP contains a serious error: the way governments are expected to account for public investment. Correcting this error […] applying the rules of the SGP to the budget inclusive of nominal interest payments and of capital depreciation, but excluding net investment, would have several desirable characteristics" (O. Blanchard, F. Giavazzi, *Improving the SGP through a Proper Accounting of Public Investment*, CEPR Discussion Paper, No. 4220, 2004, p. 3).

These theories are largely unrealistic and, as a matter of fact, it is easier to explain the political consensus for the approval of the Fiscal Compact as a product of fears generated by an increasing size of the stock of debt in some Member States, that has worsened the crisis of sovereign debt after the explosion of the financial crisis following the failure of Lehman Brothers on 15 September 2008. Nowadays, Eurozone states are not only constrained in quantitative terms, but they have also largely given up their sovereignty on budgetary issues, since they must submit a draft budget for prior approval by the European institutions. If commitments made when the budget is approved are not satisfied, the rules foresee sanctions and, in the last resort, an appeal to the European Court of Justice. The launch of this budgetary Union was strongly supported by the German government, but a balanced budget and a progressive contraction of the stock of debt are not sufficient by themselves to promote a high growth rate for the European economy. The institutional changes needed to guarantee the development of fully-fledged democracy in Europe, which could justify such a profound centralisation of fiscal policy decisions at the European level, are still missing.

6. The need for quantitative limits on the deficit

The need to impose quantitative constraints on the size of the deficit within the Monetary Union appears, at first, to be justified by the fact that quantitative restrictions on the debt capacity at lower government levels exist in almost all countries with a decentralised tax structure. Article 104C of the Treaty of Maastricht clearly established that "…the Member States must avoid excessive public deficits…", and this disposition complemented the one in Article 105(1) which solemnly reaffirmed the principle that "…the objective of the European system of central banks is to maintain price stability…".

To attain this objective the Treaty considered it essential that debt was not to be covered by money supply increases; to this end, Article 21 of the Protocol on the Statute of the European System of Central Banks and of the European Central Bank – pursuant to provisions in Article 123 of the TFEU – absolutely excludes that the European Central Bank can buy public debt bonds offered by state, regional or local administrations, or other public sector authorities of the Member States. This normative provision was strengthened by Article 125, which stated that neither the Union nor the Member States could be asked to respond "…to the commitments of central governments, regional, local or other public authorities, other bodies governed by public law, or public undertakings of any Member States...".

Now known as the no bail-out clause, this should avoid the delivery of negative externalities linked to irresponsible financial behaviour by Member States; in particular, it was meant to avoid the danger that Member States in the Union – working on the assumption that there would be support from the European Central Bank as a lender of last resort – would permit an excess emission of public debt bonds. This excess supply could cause an increase in interest rates on the whole European financial market as a result of the fall in value of the securities, while the budget balance of the state in question would become even more serious as a consequence of the increase in interest rates.

But the Maastricht Treaty also provided for a procedure to avoid excessive deficits, thereby demonstrating a lack of trust in the effectiveness of the no bail-out clause. Eichengreen and von Hagen[18] contest the necessity of this additional condition, since the bail-out problem basically only involves those countries without their own taxing capacity. In fact, in this case, if the country in question were to face a recession, there would be a strong impact on the budget, and the local government, not being able to impose its own taxes, would be faced with a serious financial crisis. The central government would then have to choose whether or not to let the local government fail or to assist it with its own means. In short, "... different models of vertical tax structures differ in the bail-out risk they entail. The stronger the dependence of the sub-central governments on the resources of the central government, the greater the bail-out risk..." and, at the same time, "...the stronger is the incentive for an excessive deficit because of the assumption of a bail-out by the central government if a financial crisis should occur...".

Eichengreen and von Hagen also point out that if political union were to be achieved, the fiscal powers of the Union would be strengthened and, as a result, "...political integration might increase the bail-out risk rather than lower it, thereby leaving the member-state governments without any other option than to turn to the European Central Bank for aid. This implies that there will be room for fiscal constraints in the future, when political unification is achieved and fiscal powers will be centralised in the European Union...". But for the moment these constraints – in their opinion – were superfluous.

---

18 B. Eichengreen, J. von Hagen, *Fiscal Restrictions and Monetary Union: Rationales, Repercussions, Reforms*, Saarbrucken, 2-3 October 1995, pp. 23-26.

The reasoning of Eichengreen and von Hagen appears to be correct, in theory. A structure of fiscal federalism increases the responsibility of the lower government levels, and normally deficits are much more restrained.[19] If, conversely, centralisation increases, local governments tend to behave as free-riders, and there is a growing risk of negative external effects on the integrated financial market. Thus, imposing constraints on the finances of the lower government levels appears to be justified.

But, in reality, the European situation is different from the theoretical model of fiscal federalism because, on the one hand, national governments have substantial fiscal autonomy – even if over time the constraints imposed by the process of tax harmonisation tend to increase – while, on the other hand, the Union has a limited power of control on Member States' behaviour, that exists in states with an effective federal structure. The absence of this power of control and direction – that is, of a real government ruling the economy – must be balanced by the imposition of *ex ante* constraints, which are part of the Treaty of Maastricht.

Eichengreen and von Hagen's conclusion can thus be reversed: in a federal state financial autonomy at lower levels of government is perhaps limited – even if in the European context it will certainly be less centralised in comparison with existing federations –, but the power of control over Member States' finances is strengthened and thus, at the same time, the bail-out risk is reduced. This should in future be the rule to be adopted in Europe, when a federal government is in place: less *ex ante* constraints on fiscal behaviour of Member States, but strengthened control on the overall fiscal stance within the Monetary Union.

---

19 W. Moesen, P. van Rompuy, *The Growth of Government Size and Fiscal Decentralization*, Paper prepared for Iipf Congress, Brussels, 1990.

Chapter 3

The structure of the Monetary Union

1. The degree of centralisation within the Monetary Union

One important feature of the evolution of the Monetary Union is made clear in this quotation:[20]

> the Fiscal Compact systematically enhances the powers of the EU institutions to direct and police the budgetary policies of the states, thus increasing centralisation in the EU architecture of economic governance. This development contrasts with the federal experience of the United States (US). In fact, it appears that while most US states are also endowed with *golden rules* in their constitutions, the federal government never played a role in the adoption of these balanced budget rules and still today is barred from interfering with the budgetary processes of the states.

According to this remark, an unexpected paradox emerges in the institutional architecture of the EU. When the crisis exploded in 2008, European governments rejected a US-like federal model as being too centralised for the EU, but they have ended up establishing a regime that is much less respectful of state sovereignty than the US federal system. The reason for this apparent paradox is simple. In the United States the federal government is endowed, in the areas where it has a competence, with an effective capacity of taking decisions, approved by the Congress and the Senate, where Member States are represented. Hence, a federal decision is founded on a democratic process and could reasonably be enforced on Member States. But they keep their sovereignty where the competence is not attributed to the federal level, which cannot interfere with Member States in their exercise of management of policy decisions.

[20] F. Fabbrini, *The fiscal compact, the "Golden Rule", and the paradox of European federalism*, Tilburg Law School Legal Studies Research Paper Series, No. 013/2013.

Within the Monetary Union, by relying on strict and detailed balanced-budget rules mandated by the Fiscal Compact, the Commission will not only control compliance with the constraints of the Stability Pact, but will also be able to implement a more pervasive *ex ante* scrutiny on the sustainability and appropriateness of the draft budget bills which governments submit for approval during the European Semester. In the end, it emerges that the Fiscal Compact, with its balanced-budget requirement, adds another stone to the path of increasing centralisation in the EU, but without the guarantees of a fully-fledged federal structure gained through appropriate *checks and balances*. Furthermore, it must be critically underlined that these developments do not fully involve the European Parliament, which does not play a central role in this new structure of the Union, weakening the legitimacy of the transfer of growing portions of decision-making to the EU level.

The conclusion that it is possible to draw from these remarks seems straightforward: from one side, the economic crisis has highlighted the lack of effective decision-making power at the European level. The only timely and effective measures to promote the recovery of the European economy, after the start of the crisis in 2008, were implemented by the ECB, a federal institution; in all the other cases, decisions were only taken by the Council after a lengthy process, with greater costs and less effectiveness. But, at the same time, the fiscal sovereignty of Member States, in defining their budget priorities, has been substantially constrained through the European Semester procedure and by the rules of the Fiscal Compact. While EU Member States' governments have systematically rejected calls in favour of a federal arrangement for the EMU, as being disrespectful of State sovereignty, they have established a regime for the governance of the Monetary Union that sacrifices State sovereignty much more than would have been permitted in a federal system.

In order to bring efficiency and democracy together in the field of European economic policy, the recipe to follow is simple: less binding and automatic rules, and more effective discretional decision power at the European level – including the power to enforce decisions once they have been taken. But the decision process should be radically changed, recognising the role of the Commission as the effective government of the Union and including not only the Ministers of Member States' governments, in a Council where majority vote is the general rule, but also the European Parliament. In contrast, less interference should be guaranteed in national decision-making processes in the areas where the competence is left to the Member States, following the subsidiarity principle. The implication of this evolution in the economic and monetary field will be a decisive step towards a federal system, less centralised than the current one, but, at the same time, more efficient and democratic.

2. Reform proposals of EMU governance

In recent years reforms of the Economic and Monetary Union's governance have been the subject of important contributions by the Presidents of the European institutions. In a Report signed by the five Presidents[21] the direction of travel was made clear: "…for the euro area to gradually evolve towards a genuine Economic and Monetary Union, it will need to shift from a system of rules and guidelines for national economic policy-making to a system of further sovereignty sharing within common institutions, most of which already exists and can progressively fulfil the task…". But this evolution, in their evaluation, is something for the future, since in Stage 1 this document only envisages, as a move towards a Fiscal Union, the creation of an Advisory Fiscal Board and, in Stage 2, a vague stabilisation mechanism to cushion macroeconomic shocks.

An earlier Report of the Presidents[22] included an important paragraph entitled *Towards a fiscal capacity for the EMU* in which it noted that

> while the degree of centralisation of budgetary instruments and the arrangements for fiscal solidarity against adverse shocks differ, all other currency unions are endowed with a central fiscal capacity. In this respect, the European Council in October 2012 asked to explore further mechanisms, including an *appropriate fiscal capacity*, for the euro area. It would support new functions which are not covered by the multi-annual financial framework from which it is clearly separated

This should be the right path to follow.[23] But, instead, the basic idea underlying the Five Presidents' Report is that, in the short run, the recovery of the euro area only requires a more efficient coordination of national

---

21 *The Five Presidents' Report: Completing Europe's Economic and Monetary Union*, Brussels, 22 June 2015.

22 *Towards a genuine Economic and Monetary Union*, Report by the President of the European Council, Brussels, 5 December 2012.

23 "The only governance that can be sustained in the eurozone is one where a eurozone government backed by a European Parliament acquires the power to tax and spend. Put differently, the eurozone can only be sustained if it is embedded in a fiscal and political union" (P. De Grauwe, *Macroeconomic Policies in the Eurozone since the Sovereign Debt Crisis*, Policy Paper No. 13, Euroforum KU Leuven, September 2014, p. 20).

economic policies, with a stronger focus on employment and social performance (that is naturally highly desirable). Since, according to their view, euro-area governance is already well established for the coordination and surveillance of fiscal policies, the next step should be limited to the creation of a euro-area system of Competitiveness Authority.

Some progress has been made, EU economic policy coordination has been strengthened with the introduction of the European Semester, in 2010, and the toolbox for EU level economic governance has been improved with the creation of National Productivity Boards and a European Fiscal Board. However, the euro-area architecture is not yet complete. A further contribution was provided by a Reflection Paper[24] of the European Commission that followed and developed ideas put forward by a previous White Paper.[25]

The most relevant new ideas in these papers proposed the creation of a European safe asset, a new financial instrument for the common issuance of debt, which would reinforce integration and financial stability, and envisage the establishment of a macroeconomic stabilisation instrument for the euro area. Guiding principles for this instrument – it should not lead to permanent transfers or duplicate the role of the European Stability Mechanism, while minimising the risks of moral hazard – were already specified in the Five Presidents' Report.

In a further Communication,[26] the Commission discussed four specific functions that are considered essential for the deepening of the Economic and Monetary Union. It proposed as concrete next steps: a) support to structural reforms in Member States; b) a dedicated convergence facility for Member States on their way to joining the euro; c) a backstop for the Banking Union, through the European Stability Mechanism (that should become a European Monetary Fund); d) a stabilisation function, bringing together different EU and euro area level funds and financial instruments, to be used to maintain investment levels in the event of large asymmetric shocks.

It must be recognised that while some steps forward are foreseen in these proposals, as monetary policy is fully centralised, other instruments of economic policy have remained largely in the hands of the national

---

24 European Commission, *Reflection Paper on the Deepening of the Economic and Monetary Union*, COM(2017) 291, Brussels, 31 May 2017.

25 European Commission, *White Paper on the Future of Europe. Reflections and Scenarios for the EU27 by 2025*, Brussels, 1 March 2017.

26 European Commission, *Further Steps towards Completing Europe's Economic and Monetary Union: a Roadmap*, COM(2017) 821 final, Brussels, 6 December 2017.

governments. This is a serious design failure. Ideally, countries should share the use of these instruments with European institutions, recognising the power of the European Commission to rule effectively the coordination of stabilisation and growth policy with Member States. However, the willingness to take such a drastic step towards political union appears generally weak.[27]

It seems largely reasonable to envisage that some instruments of economic policy, particularly in the field of fiscal policy, should be attributed to the European level. The Union is facing the threat of terrorism, the inflow of millions of migrants and political disorder in the Mediterranean area, and a difficult transition to a new model of growth in a globalised economy. Given these dramatic conditions it appears more and more urgent to attribute to the Union and, at least partially to the Eurozone, a real power for collecting the larger amount of resources that are needed to finance the new expenditures necessary to tackle the challenges currently confronting Europe.

3. A new fiscal architecture of the Eurozone

A paper prepared by 14 French and German economists[28] represents a significant contribution to the debate on the reform of the Eurozone. Drawing on many previous proposals of the European Commission, this paper deals with different aspects of the Eurozone issue, starting from ideas for completing the Banking Union, strengthening the bank resolution regime, reducing the exposure of banks to their domestic sovereigns, creating a European deposit insurance scheme and removing disincentives to the geographic diversification of bank assets beyond their home country. All these proposals should be managed with care since, in the presence of high legacy debts, a more stringent market discipline could backfire unless effective risk sharing arrangements are put in place at the same time.

But their analysis mainly focused on the EU's fiscal architecture, putting forward significant suggestions. Existing rules were considered important, but open to criticism. The goal of reducing the amount of deficit engenders corresponding pro-cyclical effects, favouring an increase in expenditure during boom periods and a reduction following a downturn.

---

27 P. De Grauwe, "The Governance of a Fragile Eurozone", in *Australian Economic Review*, September 2012, pp. 255-262.

28 A. Bénassi-Quéré *et al.*, *Reconciling risk-sharing with market discipline: A constructive approach to euro area reform*, CEPR Policy Insight, No. 91, January 2018.

It is true that the deficit should be measured with due consideration of the trend of the cycle, but this evaluation is notoriously difficult and inaccurate. In respect of the implementation of the rules, this should be made effective by imposing fines, that thus far have never been utilised and, moreover, will worsen an already difficult financial condition. But rules are needed, not only to guarantee sound national finances, but also to avoid negative external effects on the other members of the Monetary Union.

The first proposal put on the table by the French-German economists derives from the idea that rules for ceilings put on nominal public expenditure growth, consistent with public debt reduction targets, are better than existing constraints on the amount of deficit. The basic principle underlying an expenditure rule[29] implies that nominal expenditures should not grow faster than long-term nominal income (the sum of potential output growth and expected inflation) and at a slower pace in countries that need to reduce their debts. Each year, an independent national-level fiscal council should propose a rolling medium-term debt reduction target and a medium-term nominal growth projection. Then, the same council would chart a consistent medium-term nominal expenditure path and use it to set a nominal expenditure ceiling, net of interest payments, of unemployment spending and of the estimated impact of any new discretionary revenue measures, to preclude the manipulation of tax rules that are not compensated by offsetting expenditure measures.

If a country were to pass a budget with spending above the target, all excessive spending would have to be financed by junior sovereign bonds, the first to be restructured in case a debt reduction is deemed necessary to ensure sustainability, and containing a clause that specifies an automatic maturity extension if the country receives a ESM-supported conditional assistance programme. Furthermore, junior bonds would not benefit from existing regulatory privileges of sovereign debt, *e.g.* zero risk-weighting, normally granted to senior bonds held in bank portfolios. This provision would increase the cost of financing excess debt, creating a disincentive to behaviours not aligned with the target of cutting down the deficit and

[29] A reference to an expenditure benchmark has been already introduced as part of the 2011 reforms (the Six Pack). The benchmark is a rule which contains the net growth rate of government spending at or below a country's medium-term potential economic growth rate, depending on the country's position in relation to its medium-term budgetary objectives (MTO). Under the expenditure benchmark, spending increases which go beyond a country's medium-term potential economic growth rate must be matched by additional discretionary revenue measures. The expenditure benchmark complements the MTO by putting growth in net expenditure on a sustainable path and therefore helping to move towards or maintain the MTO itself.

the stock of debt, and seems to be in line with the content of a Directive recently proposed by the European Commission.[30]

The second relevant suggestion included in this paper proposed the creation of a fiscal stabilisation scheme that would offer one-off transfers, in the case of large downturns affecting one or several member states, and would help stabilise the cycle, overcoming the limits of EMS funds that are available only in exceptional cases. There are at least four important features of this proposal to be underlined.

First, it would be designed as a reinsurance fund for large shocks affecting the labour market in euro area countries, and could be conceived as a line in the EU budget or as a subsidiary of the EMS. Reinsurance means that covering the first loss associated with a particular shock remains the responsibility of the country itself. Second, the fiscal stabilisation instrument should be linked to employment-based indicators (changes in the unemployment rate, employment, wage bill), that are observed more easily than real GDP. Third, there would be a one-time transfer of a fixed percentage of national GDP for each percentage point increase in unemployment or decline in employment or in the wage bill, beyond the specified threshold. Lastly, the system would be financed through national contributions (annually 0.1% of GDP), dependant on the volatility of the variable that is used to define the trigger, since this determines the probability that the country will need a pay-out from the fund; the higher that probability, the higher the contribution. These characteristics should keep out moral hazard risks and would prove a disincentive to irresponsible fiscal behaviour by the Eurozone's Member States.

The third important proposal included in the paper related to the creation of a Euro area safe asset backed by sovereign bonds.[31] On this point, a significant technical contribution was provided by a paper of the European Systemic Risk Board.[32] In this proposal safety is achieved as financial intermediaries would purchase a standardised diversified portfolio of sovereign bonds, not including any junior sovereign bonds, and use this as a collateral for a security issued in several tranches, calibrated so that the five-year expected yield of the most senior tranche – referred

---

30 European Commission, *Proposal for a Council Directive laying down provisions for strengthening fiscal responsibility and the medium-term budgetary orientation in the Member States*, COM(2017) 824 final, 6 December 2017.

31 European Commission, *Reflection Paper on the Deepening of the Economic and Monetary Union*, COM(2017) 291, Brussels, 31 May 2017, p. 22.

32 European Systemic Risk Board, *ESBies; Safety in tranches*, ESRB, Working Paper Series, No. 21, September 2016.

to as European Senior Bonds, or ESBies – is about the same as that of a AAA-rated sovereign bond. Assets of this type should both be attractive to banks trying to reduce concentrated sovereign exposures, and create demand for the bonds of these sovereigns, reducing the impact of shifts in market sentiment against vulnerable euro area members, helping them to maintain market access and avoid sharp spikes in borrowing costs.

The Commission advanced a proposal[33] for the creation of sovereign bond-backed securities (SBBS), which would be a new type of asset created by the private sector, based on an underlying portfolio including sovereign bonds of all euro area Member States, with relative weights in line with each Member State's contribution to the capital of European Central Bank.[34] A private sector entity would assemble a portfolio of euro area sovereign bonds from the market and subsequently transfer them to a legally separate, self-standing entity, specifically set up for the sole purpose of issuing to investors a series of higher or lower risk securities representing claims from this underlying portfolio. The highest-risk (junior) securities would be the first in line to bear any losses on the underlying pool, should they arise, but would in exchange pay investors a higher return. Senior securities would be low-risk, as they would bear losses only after junior securities have been completely wiped out to absorb the losses. The size of the senior tranche would be fixed at 70% of the whole SBBS issue, ensuring that it is as safe as the least risky euro area sovereign bonds.

The package of proposals of the 14 Franco-German economists seems adequate to foster an improvement of the fiscal architecture of the euro area, reconciling risk sharing with market discipline. From the institutional viewpoint, a strong backing is provided in the paper to the idea put forward by Juncker,[35] supported by Emmanuel Macron,[36] to create a new Eurozone

---

33 European Commission, *Proposal for a Regulation on Sovereign Bond-Backed Securities*, Brussels, 24 May 2018, COM(2018) 339 final.

34 "The key to be considered a safe asset is, of course, sound fiscal and structural policy. A pool of euro-area bonds can contribute to diversify risks, but faces numerous drawbacks. The SBBS idea remains untested and politically controversial" (G. Claeys, *Are SBBS really the safe asset the euro area is looking for?*, Brueghel Blog Post, 28 May 2018).

35 J.C. Juncker, *State of the Union's Address 2017*, Brussels, 13 September 2017. This proposal has been formally included in the Commission's roadmap (European Commission, *Further steps towards completing the Economic and Monetary Union: a roadmap*, COM(2017) 821 final, Brussels, 6 December 2017) and has been fully clarified in: European Commission, *A European Minister of Economy and Finance*, COM(2017) 823 final, Brussels, 6 December 2017.

36 *Initiative pour l'Europe.* Discours d'Emmanuel Macron: *Pour une Europe souveraine, unie, démocratique*, Paris, 26 Septembre 2017.

Economy and Finance Minister. Following the double-hat model, as is the case for the Union's High Representative for Foreign Affairs and Security Policy, the Minister would take part in the Commission and chair the Eurogroup, and would be answerable to the European Parliament, controlling the implementation of fiscal rules and defining the fiscal stance for the whole area, while representing the Eurozone at the international level.

A radical criticism of these ideas has been advanced by Messori and Micossi,[37] who argue that the proposals of the French and German economists "…do not differ in substance from Schäuble's[38] on the critical issue of financial stability in the euro area and the balance between risk reduction and risk sharing, and in some respect even more rigid…". Their remarks relate in particular to the Banking Union, the EMS's tasks and sovereign debts. But the main point seems to be a criticism of the fiscal discipline in the version proposed by the French-German economists, regarding both fiscal rules centred on sovereign debt reduction with a ceiling on public expenditure, managed either by national fiscal councils and European Fiscal Board or by the ESM, and a rainy-day fund to provide one-off transfers for large labour market shocks.[39]

Pisani-Ferry and Zettelmeyer's reply[40] mainly concerns this institutional issue since, while Messori and Micossi suggest that the French-German "…transparent objective is not only to exclude the Commission from any role in negotiating policy goals with member states within the European semester procedures…", they envisage a model where Commissioners would be responsible for both economic and fiscal monitoring, and the forging of political compromises, which would actually lead to the transfer of the chair of the Eurogroup from the Council to the Commission. This could be a reasonable compromise between efficiency and democracy, if adequate protection from undue political interference were guaranteed to a fiscal watchdog located within the Commission. One advantage of this model is that it could be implemented without major treaty changes, since the Commission is already currently involved in fiscal surveillance.

---

37 M. Messori, S. Micossi, *Counterproductive Proposals on Euro Area Reform by French and German Economists*, CEPS Policy Insights, No. 2018-04/ February 2018.

38 W. Schäuble, *Non-paper for paving the way towards a Stability Union*, 2017.

39 This suggestion has been advocated in various forms by the European Commission (European Commission, *Reflection Paper on the Deepening of Economic and Monetary Union*, Brussels, 31 May 2017) and some Member States (Italian Position Paper, *Reforming the European Monetary Union in a stronger European Union*, Rome, 13 December 2017).

40 J. Pisani-Ferry, J. Zettelmeyer, *Messori and Micossi's reading of the Franco-German 7+7 paper is a misrepresentation*, CEPS Commentary, 19 February 2018.

Another important contribution to the debate on the fiscal architecture of the Eurozone came from IMF Managing Director Christine Lagarde.[41] Following proposals to complete the Capital Market Union, and to prevent other crises in the banking sector through the creation of a common deposit insurance scheme and a shared fiscal backstop for the Single Resolution Fund, she turned her attention to fiscal issues, stressing that the main role in facing the last crisis was played by monetary policy, while raising taxes and cutting spending – as many in the euro area did between 2011-2013 – exacerbated weaknesses and contributed to a double-dip recession. Therefore, she emphasised that "…to avoid a painful repeat of this experience, the euro area needs a central fiscal capacity…". This central fiscal capacity would reassure investors that the euro area will have better tools to stop the next crisis from spreading and could help smooth out the economic cycle, especially when monetary policy proves insufficient.[42]

In this perspective Lagarde recalled that in a paper presented by the IMF[43] the creation of a *rainy-day fund* was suggested, to which countries contribute every year, building up assets in good times so that they could receive transfers to help them offset budget shortfalls in the depth of a downturn. Thus, the proposals of the IMF largely coincided with the suggestion of the 14 French and German economists. The architecture of the euro area could be improved and, in particular, the goal of fiscal stabilisation in case of asymmetric shocks be achieved. But this depends fundamentally on the capacity to reach an agreement on the creation of a fiscal capacity at the European level.

4. A budget for the Eurozone

In the current political debate proposals are frequently made to create a Eurozone budget, funded with own resources and governed by a European Minister of Economy and Finance.[44] The underlying idea is that the euro area should be provided with an instrument that could be used

41 C. Lagarde, *A Compass to Prosperity: The Next Steps of Euro Area Economic Integration*, German Institute for Economic Research, Berlin, 26 March 2018.

42 IMF, *Revisiting the Economic Case for Fiscal Union in the Euro Area*, IMF Departmental Paper, Washington, February 2018.

43 N. Arnold, B. Barkbu, E. Ture, H. Wang, J. Yao, *A Central Fiscal Stabilization Capacity for the Euro Area*, IMF Staff Discussion Note, 26 March, 2018.

44 In his third speech on the State of the Union Juncker also proposed the appointment of a European Minister of Economy and Finance (J.C. Juncker, *State of the Union's Address 2017*, Brussels, 13 September 2017). This proposal has been included formally in the roadmap presented by the Commission (European Commission, *Further Steps*

for anti-cyclical purposes if new deflationary crises were to appear in the future, in order to ensure the stability of the common currency as well as a recovery of growth and employment. At the same time, the Eurozone should dispose of the resources needed to guarantee internal and external security, to support the structural changes brought about by technological innovations and by an organic transition to sustainable development – so that the external competitiveness of the European firms is guaranteed in a globalised world – and to promote the full employment of the labour force, backed by an adequate level of wages.

Post-Brexit the idea of creating a separate budget for the Eurozone, in order to strengthen the functioning of the Economic and Monetary Union, would appear to be more realistic. Currently, according to the Treaty, with the exception of the United Kingdom and Denmark,[45] all Member States of the European Union are obliged to join the euro area in due time, and thus have an interest in increasing the strength of the instruments that the Eurozone has at its disposal.[46]

The European Commission recognises now that there is widespread support for the idea that "…mechanisms should be set up to allow euro area Member States to take decisions amongst themselves, with a strengthening of the Eurogroup, and in the European Parliament…", even if it underlines that "…this question might be less of an issue as more Member States join the euro area over time…".[47] But, if in the medium term the frame of reference should remain the Union's budget, "…in the meantime, transparency *vis-à-vis* current non-euro area Member States on further steps of deepening EMU is essential…".[48]

From this point there arise two, conflicting, goals. On one side, the need to move forward on the road towards a more efficient Economic

---

towards Completing Europe's Economic and Monetary Union: a Roadmap, COM(2017) 821 final, Brussels, 6 December 2017).

45 In the Edinburgh European Council (December 1992), after having kept in mind that according to the Protocol annexed to the Maastricht Treaty Denmark will not take part in the third phase of the EMU, it has been decided that "Denmark will take part fully in the second phase of the Economic and Monetary Union and will continue to take part to the cooperation in the issues related to exchange rates policy in the framework of the European Monetary System".

46 Bulgaria, that at the moment does not take part in the Monetary Union, has nonetheless anchored to the euro the value of its national currency.

47 In his State of the Union speech (September 2017) Juncker reaffirms that the euro should become the single currency for the whole European Union.

48 European Commission, *Reflection Paper on the Deepening of the Economic and Monetary Union*, COM(2017) 291, Brussels, 31 May 2017, p. 27.

and Monetary Union concerns all Member States, not just the limited group of countries that are using the euro; but, on the other side, the central role of the euro must be recognised and, at the same time, the need to reconcile the ambition of some countries to go further on the road towards *an ever closer Union*, as envisaged by the Treaty of Rome, and the respect of the rhythm preferred by each country. As such, the objective to be reached would be to guarantee new resources for a Eurozone budget, in an enlarged Union budget, to avoid those who want to hold back the process of deepening the Monetary Union from preventing the countries of the euro area progressing more rapidly, but keeping in mind that, in the medium term, all Member States of the Union should join the euro area.

In fact, a solution could be envisaged that will satisfy both these requirements, establishing that, at least partially, the own resources created in the near future to finance the European budget – and flowing from the Member States that have already joined the single currency – will be attributed to a budget line that could be used only in favour of the countries that are part of the euro area.[49] Rules governing the EU budget to date permit the establishment of a new budget heading to the benefit of some, not all, EU Members, cohesion policy being an obvious example. Revenue assignment to a specific budget line is likewise possible; such assigned revenue provides an additional advantage, since it does not fall under the GNI budgetary ceilings established by the Own Resources Regulation, whose amendment requires unanimity and ratification according to national procedures.[50]

The decision on these resources, and on their use, would be taken within the Eurogroup, chaired by a European Minister of Economy and

49 "…We do not need parallel structures. We do not need a budget for the euro area, but a strong euro area budget line within the EU budget…" (J.C. Juncker, *State of the Union's Address 2017*, Brussels, 13 September 2017. This idea has been further developed in a Commission communication on new budgetary instruments for a stable euro area within the Union framework (COM(2017) 0822). A similar argument has been put forward in the Italian Position Paper, *Reforming the European Monetary Union in a Stronger European Union*, where, after having underlined the importance of creating a *rainy-day fund* to provide a stabilisation function in the euro area, it was noted that "…from an institutional point of view, the fund should be managed by a European Treasury and could be part of a euro area budget line within the EU budget…" (p. 12). The European Parliament as well "…supports the proposal made by the President of the Commission, Jean-Claude Juncker, for the creation of a specific line dedicated to the euro area within the EU budget…" (European Parliament, *Draft Report on reform of the European Union's system of own resources*, 2017 /2053(INI), Rapporteurs G. Deprez, J. Lewandowski, Brussels, 10 January 2018, point 18).

50 European Commission, *Revenue for EMU: A contribution to the debate on Fiscal Union*, Taxation Papers, WP No. 54, 2015; R. Repasi, *Legal options for an additional EMU fiscal capacity*, European Parliament, Policy department C, Brussels, 2013.

Finance, under the control of the European Parliament. On this point a growing consensus now seems to exist. According to the Commission,[51] a European Minister of Economy and Finance could help identify and pursue an adequate fiscal policy for the euro area as a whole. As a member of the Commission, the Minister would coordinate the surveillance of Member States' fiscal policies, ensuring fiscal sustainability and applying the Stability and Growth Pact. Part of his task would also be to assess the appropriateness of the fiscal stance of the euro area, thereby contributing to finding the right balance between the fiscal interests of Member States and the best solution for the euro area as a whole. He could be elected as President of the Eurogroup with a view of seeking consensus on the broad policy direction and the overall strategy for the euro area. The Minister, as a member of the Commission, would be accountable to the European Parliament on all issues related to his functions.

Recently an important contribution to the euro area reform proposals was the Meseberg Declaration signed by Emmanuel Macron and Angela Merkel.[52] After underlining that "...France and Germany share a common ambition for the European project: a democratic, sovereign and united Europe...", they proposed "...establishing a Eurozone budget within the framework of the European Union to promote competitiveness, convergence and stabilisation in the euro area, starting in 2021...". Resources for this budget would come both from national contributions, allocation of tax revenues and European resources. The main purpose of the Eurozone budget would be to guarantee competitiveness and convergence, which would be delivered through investment in innovation and human capital. The issue of a European Unemployment Stabilization Fund should be examined as well. Strategic decisions on the Eurozone budget would be taken by the Eurozone countries, while decisions on expenditures should be executed by the European Commission.

The creation of a budget line within the EU budget, exclusively devoted to supporting initiatives in favour of euro area Member States and the institution of an Economy and Finance Minister, would be an important step forward on the path towards a complete and efficient Fiscal Union, democratically controlled by the European Parliament. This institutional development would allow countries that have already joined the Monetary Union to proceed on the road towards deeper integration,

---

51 European Commission, *A European Minister of Economy and Finance*, COM(2017) 823 final, Brussels, 6 December 2017.

52 *Renewing Europe's promises of security and prosperity*, The Press and Information Office of the Federal Government, 19 June 2018.

without creating a barrier to other Member States that, in the long term, will be obliged to join the euro. But the central issue to be faced concerns the powers granted to the European Commission in defining the fiscal stance of the whole European economy, the size of the EU budget, and the amount of real own resources that should guarantee the financing of expenditures needed to face the new tasks that the European Union must fulfil, *vis-à-vis* the challenges deriving from security issues, worldwide competition and technological innovations in a globalised world.

5. A revised structure of the EU budget

An important point emerging from the previous analysis concerns the size of the EU budget. If broad responsibility for stabilisation policy is to be assigned to the European level, but an important role continues to be played through the coordination of national budgets – and, in the future, it can be foreseen that also the role of the sub-national budgets in stabilisation policy will increase –, then the size of the EU budget can be much lower compared to the previous experience of federal states. In effect, it seems possible to achieve the objectives of the EMU with a limited-sized budget, equal to around 2-2.5% of European GDP, which includes a reserve of around 0.2-0.35% of GDP, set aside for the regional stabilisation mechanism.[53]

As such, the indications of the MacDougall Report, which called for a budget equalling 5-7% of European GDP in the event of a complete Monetary Union, are not being adhered to, at least up to the point where a large part of defence expenditures are attributed to the EU budget. But, before establishing the optimal size of the EU budget, it is useful to define the framework, the structure of the budget, underlining the role of different expenditures and, consequently, what should be the resources targeted to financing the single types of expenditure.

A budget structure that seems best suited to this scope[54] foresees a first Chapter (Transfers between Member States) that will include Structural

---

[53] The first figure has been estimated by A. Italianer, M. Vanheukelen, "Proposals for Community Stabilization Mechanisms: Some Historical Applications", in *European Economy: Reports and Studies*, 1993, No. 5, pp. 493-510, the second is the amount considered necessary by N. Arnold, B. Barkbu, E. Ture, H. Wang, J. Yao, *A Central Fiscal Stabilization Capacity for the Euro Area*, IMF Staff Discussion Note, 26 March 2018.

[54] A. Iozzo, S. Micossi, M.T. Salvemini, *A new budget for the European Union?*, CEPS Policy Brief, No. 159, May 2008.

Funds, the Cohesion Fund and direct payments to farmers for supporting their level of income. Since these expenditures are mainly of redistributive character, it seems reasonable that they could continue to be financed through national contributions proportional to the GDP level of each country.

The second Chapter (European public goods), is more important, and innovative; it should finance economic and growth policies (policy for the internal market and structural agricultural policy, but mainly R&D programs, technological innovation, environmental policy, social measures to overcome the difficult transition towards a post-industrial economy), internal security and control of migration, foreign policy, common defence, administrative expenditures and interest paid on bonds emitted by the Union. These expenditures, that represent the core of the Union's new policy to face the main challenges with which Europe is confronted, should be funded not only with traditional own resources (VAT, custom duties) that are totally insufficient, but with new own resources that should be introduced to pave the way towards a European public finance. A third Chapter could include capital expenditures, mainly investment for common European projects (for instance, Galileo) that could be funded through bonds placed in the market.

As foreseen in existing Treaties,[55] "...the revenue and expenditure shown in the budget shall be in balance...". But the own resource ceiling in the current MFF[56] could reach 1.23% of European GNI, with a large margin available towards payment appropriations, whose percentage of GNI declines from 0.98% in 2014 to 0.91% in 2020.[57] If the difference between this ceiling and the effective payments could be fully exploited, the size of the EU budget could be increased immediately by between 0.25% and 0.33%. In this way a gradual and progressive reform of the Union's budget could be promoted, keeping in mind in any case that the literature on the optimal size of the Monetary Union[58] suggests that

---

55 This rule is included in Article 310 of the Treaty on the Functioning of the European Union.

56 Council Regulation No. 1311/2013 of 2 December 2013 laying down the multiannual financial framework for the years 2014-2020.

57 While this is the maximum amount of payment appropriations foreseen in the current MFF, commitment appropriations decline during the 7 years period of the last MFF from 1.03% to 0.98% of the GNI of the Union.

58 Commission of the European Communities, *Report of the Study Group on the Role of Public Finance in European Integration*, Brussels, April 1977; European Commission, "Stable Money, Sound Finances. Community Public Finance in the Perspective of EMU", in *European Economy*, Brussels, 1993, No. 53.

in due time the budget should reach a level equal at least to 2-2.5% of European GDP.

6. A reform of the Multiannual Financial Framework

According to Article 312 of the TFEU, "...the annual budget of the Union shall comply with the Multiannual Financial Framework...". The timeframe of the MFF has, until now, been 7 years, but the Treaty of Lisbon states that "...it shall be established for a period of at least five years..." (Article 312). If this became the normal length of the MFF, "...a 5-year timeframe would align with the mandates of the European Parliament and the Commission. This would strengthen the democratic debate on the EU's spending priorities and put the EU budget more clearly at the centre of European politics...".[59]

Besides the issue of the timeframe, the MFF – that fixes the limits of the yearly EU budget – should be in future approved with a reformed procedure that will involve the two tiers of government that are directly interested in the definition of the choices on financial policy – the European and the national – within a mechanism of a federal nature. This mechanism would foresee a proposal by the Commission and a final decision with a qualified majority vote in a common session of the Council and of the European Parliament. With this renewed procedure,[60] at the beginning of each legislature the Commission would make its proposal on the structure of the MFF, taking into account the ideas emerging during the European electoral process. The second step would be for the proposal to be discussed and evaluated with a qualified majority in a Fiscal Convention, where the European Parliament and the 27 National Parliaments would be represented, so that the different options for the financing of the Union could be the object of an in-depth discussion among the political and social forces at different levels. Given the relevance of the MFF, that rigidly fixes the limits of yearly budgetary choices, the final approval would be assumed with a qualified majority in a common extraordinary session of the Council and the European Parliament.[61]

---

59 European Commission, *Reflection Paper on the Future of EU Finances*, Brussels, 28 June 2017, p. 26.

60 A. Iozzo, *Aspetti istituzionali della procedura di adozione del Multiannual Financial Framework: un nuovo contesto per il 2021-2027*, Centro Studi sul Federalismo, Torino, 2018.

61 "The inadequacy of the traditional model of a federal state, based on the tax autonomy of each tier of government, is shown from the ensuing competition between European

With this procedure, the elaboration and approval of the choices related to the distribution of fiscal resources, and the assignment of expenditures to different sectors, could be shared among the different tiers of government, and this innovation would represent a fundamental feature of modern systems of fiscal federalism.[62] In reality, if the decision on financial choices were ultimately given to the Council – even if after obtaining the consent of the European Parliament – as it is now the case, and require a unanimity vote, the procedure would remain at the level of inter-governmental cooperation; it would not promote the pursuit of a real European added value in budgetary choices. On the contrary, if the final decision were in the hands of the European Parliament, with a minor role given to the Council, a dangerous tendency to centralisation could prevail, with the concomitant sacrifice of the interests of Member States.

Furthermore, the distribution among different levels can neither be decided on the basis of the nature of each tax – reserving for instance some taxes to the lower tiers of government due to the relative immobility of the tax base – since this solution cannot guarantee that the growth rate of the revenues will be adequate to support the allocative goals that should be achieved, nor on the basis of fixed quantitative limits, that is with constraints that could obstacle the possibility to shape the economic policy according to the needs of the economic cycle.

An efficient system of fiscal federalism requires the final decision on the distribution of fiscal resources, among the different tiers of government, to represent the focus of a plan where the fundamental choices over the economic life of the Union and of the Member States converge. In such a context, in decisions regarding the fiscal plan the European Parliament,

---

and national tax authorities which, confronted with the limit represented by the taxable income of the taxpayers, will reach an equilibrium point only with the subordination of the weakest level to the strongest one. In a modern federal system the solution of the problem of distributing tax revenues can be conferred neither to a single level of government, nor to the competition among the different levels, but must be attributed to an ad hoc institution that could be a common session of the Council representing the States and the Parliament representing the citizens" (F. Rossollillo, *Città, territorio, istituzioni nella società post-industriale*, Napoli, Guida Editori, 1983, pp. 70-72).

62 "The only way to avoid the predominance of a level of government on the others is to entrust the decision on the distribution of the financial means to the only institution where both the needs of the Union and of the Member States can be taken into account: an institution where the Council and the Parliament decide together. With this procedure at the beginning of each legislature the relevant economic goals of the following five years could be established, deciding at the same time the distribution of resources needed to achieve these goals" (M. Albertini, "La proposta del MFE per il dibattito sulla riforma istituzionale della Comunità", in *Il Federalista*, 1981, n. 2).

representing the citizens, and the Council, representing the governments of the Member States, should take part on an equal footing.

A true federal solution overcomes the limitations of the two options considered above – the inter-governmental, or the attribution of the final word on budgetary choices to the European Parliament – since the choice of fiscal federalism would require, at the end of the decision process, a joint approval of both the European and national level of government. The financial plan will thus in practice acquire a constitutional nature, representing a guarantee that a fiscal policy will be implemented that will neither damage the Union's interests, nor those of the Member States.

7. The increase in the size of the EU budget

The MFF 2014-2020 foresees a reduction of the ceiling to commitment appropriations from 1.03% of GNI of Member States in 2014, to 0.98% in 2020. Over time, the composition of the EU budget has evolved. The share of spending on agriculture and cohesion, through funding for the Common Agricultural Policy and Cohesion Policy has reduced moderately – both by around 5%, although this still accounts for around 70% of the total budget. Investment is now increasingly focused on programmes directly managed at the European level, in areas such as research and innovation, trans-European transport and energy networks, mobility programmes for young people and Europe's external action.

For the 2021-27 period the Commission proposal[63] implies a long-term budget of €1.135 billion in commitments (expressed in 2018 prices), equivalent to 1.11% of the EU27's GNI, a slight increase compared to the previous MFF. Additional resources will be invested to fund new and pressing priorities in areas such as research and innovation, young people, the digital economy, border management, security and defence; at the same time, the Commission has examined where savings can be made and efficiency improved.

The Commission considers that a stable Economic and Monetary Union is a pre-condition for jobs, growth, investment and social fairness in the Union as a whole. This is why the Commission has proposed a new Reform Support Programme which, with an overall budget of €25 billion, will offer financial and technical assistance to all Member States for the

---

63 European Commission, *A Modern Budget for a Union that Protects, Empowers and Defends. The Multiannual Financial Framework for 2021-2027*, COM(2018) 321 final, Brussels, 2 May 2018.

pursuit of priority reforms, while a European Investment Stabilisation Function will help to maintain investment levels in the event of large asymmetric shocks. It will start in the form of loans to Member States with a guarantee under the EU budget of up to €30 billion, coupled with financial assistance to Member States to cover the costs of interest.

These changes are important and a move in the right direction; but there are still important limits in the Commission's proposals that, with the reasonable intention to be realistic, do not consider that a sufficiently large amount of new resources should be attributed to the budget if the Union really wants to improve the structure of the budget. These would open up a new scenario for the development of fiscal policy within a federal-type Union, characterised by a much more important role – in terms of resources directly used by the federal budget – for investments promoting growth and competitiveness, including the creation of new jobs of good quality especially for young people, for stabilisation policy and for supporting efficiently the ecological transition to a carbon-free economy.

But there is another aspect to consider, which more directly concerns the Union's institutional development. There will, initially, be negative reactions to the proposal to increase the size of the Union's budget to at least 2% of GDP from those Member States that will have to contribute more to the European Union in a situation where respect for Maastricht fiscal constraints already imposes large sacrifices. This reaction is understandable, since the States would bear the political cost from increased fiscal pressure, while the benefits from the expenditures would be attributed to the Union. The way out of this apparent dilemma is to grant, on the basis of the principles of fiscal federalism, an autonomous taxation power to the Union, bringing together in the decision-making process the two branches of budgetary authority – the Council and the European Parliament. In this way the political and social forces would have the chance to intervene in the process of defining the fiscal policy of the Union, which might decide on an increase in spending only to the extent that it is able to guarantee a sufficient consensus, or in order to reduce other expenditures or increase the fiscal pressure.

In short, some relevant conclusions seem to emerge from this analysis which appear to be of considerable interest for fiscal policy in the EU. In particular, it seems possible to show that a limited-sized budget would be enough to make the Union function effectively, even through the activation of a regional stabilisation fund for the economies of the euro area Member States. Moreover, a budget of at least 2% of GNI seems to be sufficient to guarantee an internal and external security and solidarity policy for the European Union and to finance the expenditures that must support the new measures foreseen in the context of a policy aimed at promoting the sustainable growth of the European economy, such as that envisaged earlier in the Delors Plan.[64]

But it is also important to reform the financing system of the EU budget. All these reforms, however, are conceivable only in the context of a deeply reformed Union – overcoming the democratic deficit that still remains after Lisbon. Here the European Parliament should be recognised an effective co-decision power in fiscal matters as well, in particular the power to determine – together with the Council, no longer paralysed by the veto right and without the executive power, which is reserved instead for the Commission – the revenues necessary to finance expenditures, according to classic recommendations of fiscal federalism.

As far as the development of EU finance is concerned, an increase in the amount of resources available should be envisaged in the short to medium term to support additional expenditures needed to achieve three different objectives: a) part must be set aside for structural spending to support sustainable growth and to promote social cohesion, the importance of which has been reaffirmed with the signing of the European Pillar of Social Rights in Gothenburg on 17 November 2017; b) spending on financial aids to Third World countries – in particular, African and Neighbourhood countries – must grow substantially in order for the Union to play a greater role in the international arena; c) finally, spending for research and development, as well as for the construction of the trans-European networks, must significantly increase in order to strengthen the competitiveness of European industry.

The introduction of new instruments for providing tax revenues at the Union level obviously depends on the speed at which the completion of Monetary Union is realised. The definition of these additional resources intended to finance the EU budget certainly represents an important point; but the most important aspect from the political point of view is the recognition of the Union's power to define new taxes if new expenditures are foreseen. The decision-making structure in this case must obviously be federal in nature, calling for the intervention of both branches of the budgetary authority, the European Parliament and the Council, as representatives of the Member States.

---

[64] European Commission, *Growth, Competitiveness, Employment. The Challenges and Ways Forward into the 21st Century*, White Paper, (COM(93) 700), Brussels, 5 December 1993.

Finally, two points regarding the revision of the policy concerning the Union's own resources must be strongly underlined. The first is the need – on the basis of a fundamental principle of fiscal federalism – to decide on an increase in tax revenue each time new current account expenditures are decided on, to guarantee fiscal responsibility and, thus, efficiency of the European level of government, since the current account budget should be close to balance or in surplus, while only investments could be funded with emission of bonds. The second is the urgency to guarantee that Union's tax revenue follows principles of equity, once and for all rejecting the criterion of the *juste retour* and foreseeing an evolution of tax revenue, initially towards a proportional structure, then becoming progressive in terms of the long-term tax system, so that automatic mechanisms can be implemented to favour the territorial redistribution of income as well.

8. The unavoidable institutional changes

Taken together these considerations seem to allow a first conclusion: that the development of the Monetary Union must be conceived in such a way as to permit the Union to have an effective governing capacity for the European economy. In particular, the revision of the institutional structure of the Union, which is indispensable after the limited progress made with the Treaty of Lisbon, assumes that a solution is found along the following lines:

a) the problem of undertaking a new model of sustainable development can no longer be put off, if the desire exists to promote constant growth of the European economy. The solutions will probably be different depending on conditions in each country, but it is nevertheless clear in which direction to move. The essential is to modify relative prices, to orientate the market toward solutions that favour the use of labour, and minimise the consumption of environmental resources. Until now fiscal policy in Europe has acted exactly in the opposite direction, by reducing tax on the use of natural resources and increasing fiscal pressure on the use of labour. Lowering the burden of social security contributions – in particular those weighing on unskilled labour – through tax revenues provided by a carbon tax, would achieve this shift in relative prices, thus using the market to achieve a model of growth characterised by lower unemployment and more incisive environmental protection;

b) the concrete achievement of a growth plan for the European economy along these lines obviously assumes a strengthening of the financial resources available to the Union. This needs to take into account whether completing the EMU is realistically possible, along with the achievement of the budget needed to make it function effectively – in particular, by activating a stabilisation mechanism for the economies of the euro area Member States. A budget equal to 2-2.5% of GDP should be enough to guarantee a solidarity policy inside and outside the European Union, to finance the spending needed to support the new policies of the Union, and to favour a real process of convergence among the economies of the Member States, so that a coherent context is assured for the creation of new jobs as well as for undertaking the measures needed in order to provide the appropriate adjustments in the labour market in the framework of a more incisive and effective social policy;[65]
c) the need to strengthen the role of the European Parliament in the budgetary process must be emphasised, recognising that the Parliament must share the authority on revenue decisions, according to a basic principle of fiscal federalism. All this assumes a true European government based on democratic mechanisms, in which the political parties, organised on a European scale, have the same influence as the representatives of the Member States, in the context of a true federal bicameral system. The previous analysis thus brings out the need to proceed along the road toward strengthening the federal character of the Union in order to guarantee the sustainable growth of the European economy;
d) to be successful, the policy aimed at promoting the sustainable growth of the European economy requires the collaboration of all levels of government. The subsidiarity principle, which is now fully part of European fundamental law, implies not only that some powers should be kept at the national level, but also that regions and local authorities should be used to a large extent as an optimal level of decision-making. This is certainly the case regarding an effective European growth plan, which requires cooperation among all levels of government to carry out the measures demanded. In this regard,

---

65 L. Fransen, G. del Bufalo, E. Reviglio, *Boosting Investments in social infrastructure in Europe*, Report of the High-level Task Force on investing in Social Infrastructure in Europe chaired by R. Prodi and C. Sautter, Discussion Paper 074, Brussels, 23 January 2018; O. Fontana, *Investire nelle strutture sociali dell'UE: passare dai principi all'azione*, Centro Studi sul Federalismo, Torino, Commento No. 125, 5 febbraio 2018.

the design of an effective system of fiscal federalism represents a necessary first step at the political level for giving effective responsibility to the lower levels of government and for strengthening their capacity to participate in the realisation of a new model of growth, which should characterise the European economy in the 21st century;

e) essentially, fiscal federalism presupposes that each level of government must finance itself largely through its own taxes, while maintaining at the higher level the responsibility of redistributing resources so as to guarantee adequate equality in the availability of resources over the whole European territory. In fact, only a system of this kind is able to guarantee at the same time a number of positive effects:
   - efficiency is guaranteed, since each level of government is given responsibility and can spend money only to the extent it is able to convince its citizens that the utility of this expenditure is higher than the cost of the taxes needed to finance it;
   - this mechanism represents the only true brake on the expansion of public expenditure, since for each level of government consensus is maximised if, for a given service, expenditures – and thus taxes put on behalf of their citizens – are minimised;
   - fiscal federalism also promotes equity, since it assumes an interregional redistribution of resources in order to guarantee that, for the same fiscal effort, the citizens can obtain the same level of services all over Europe.

Chapter 4

Stabilisation of the European economy

1. The policy of stabilisation of the European economy

Once Economic and Monetary Union is under way, an important first problem concerns the role European public finance must play in stabilisation policy. The existence of economic fluctuations is certainly a fact, which cannot be denied from an empirical point of view, with important deviations of production with respect to the potential of full-employment output. And if the automatic stabilisers within the economic system are weak or operate slowly, so that the macroeconomic consequences of exogenous shocks persist, there is a strong *a priori* justification for anti-cyclical stabilisation policies. These policies can no longer be effectively managed at the national level – given the degree of interdependence among the various European economies within the internal market. It is then a question of deciding if, despite the constraints that derive from the globalisation of productive process on a world scale, it is possible to have a common stabilisation policy managed at the European level.

In reality, in the current situation of the European economy, it seems reasonable to assume that the institutional rigidity and structural parameters of the aggregate demand and supply functions are such that substantial and persistent losses of welfare can result from a non-interventionist attitude towards the economic system. The justification for public intervention in the economy is still tied to the existence of market failure. In the case of stabilisation policy, the main justification is the fact that labour markets do not reach equilibrium, either through flexible wages or the migration of labour from areas where there is excess supply to those where there is excess demand. Since it does not appear that this situation will change in the short term – and the fact that it is not reasonable to excessively force territorial mobility of labour, due to the high economic and social costs that would result – it is appropriate to try to define the conditions that must be satisfied in order to optimise the structure of public intervention at the European level in order to achieve stabilisation.

Once the need for a stabilisation policy is recognised, two problems regarding EMU must be distinguished.[66] The first concerns the possibility of achieving a macroeconomic equilibrium at the European level through an efficient combination of tax and monetary measures – monetary policy in the EMU is by definition directly managed at the central level – if there are symmetric shocks that affect the European economy as a whole. In contrast, the second problem concerns the need to provide Member States with the opportunity to deal effectively with shocks that hit a single country, or general shocks with asymmetric effects on the various countries.

The problem of stabilisation of a regional economy becomes particularly important in the EMU, since the Member States no longer have the option of utilising the instruments of monetary and exchange policy, while considerable limits to fiscal policy are imposed by both the process of harmonisation, especially in the sector of indirect taxes, and through the conditions set by the Maastricht Treaty, the Stability and Growth Pact and the Fiscal Compact concerning the size of budget deficits and overall debts. A decision must therefore be made on which alternative instruments the Member States can use to re-establish equilibrium in their economic system which, following a fall in the level of demand, or an increase in the costs of production, must face a fall in output and, as a result, employment.

With regard to the European Monetary Union, the choice of the fiscal policy measure best suited to stabilise the economy is particularly relevant, especially if it is kept in mind that the Statutes of the European Central Bank establish that the management of monetary policy must in principle be targeted to guaranteeing price stability. Thus, even if the European Central Bank provides liquidity to the market, as happened during the recent crisis,[67] as far as fiscal policy is concerned, the problem which has priority is to determine if the objectives – politically defined – of stabilisation should be achieved through variations in the EU budget or through the coordination of fiscal policies managed by the Member States.

In all existing federations the task of macroeconomic stabilisation is conferred on the central government. From a theoretical point of view, the

---

66 A. Majocchi, "Politica fiscale e principio di sussidiarietà nell'Unione europea", in E. Giardina, F. Osculati, M. Rey, *Federalismo*, Franco Angeli, Milano, 1996, pp. 62-83.

67 From an institutional point of view, it is significant to show that the ECB has been able to implement an expansionary monetary policy notwithstanding the opposition of the German representative in the Governing Council since the European Central Bank is a federal institution where decisions are taken through majority voting. This unfortunately is still not the case for fiscal policy, where policy decisions require unanimity.

main justification for this is linked to the fact that, in an open economy, an important part of public expenditure will benefit non-residents through a change in imports, while residents must bear the cost from the increased future taxes needed to finance the higher level of public debt. Stabilisation thus presents elements of a public good, and, as a result, without policy measures targeted to contrast the effects of the shocks, the level of stabilisation pursued tends to be sub-optimal.

There is widespread agreement among economists on the idea that stabilisation policy must be attributed to the central government, a theory which has already been put forth by Musgrave[68] in his assignment of economic functions to public authorities. The MacDougall Report[69] followed the same lines in respect of the role of public finance in Europe. The Report came out when conditions were very different at the political level, as well as in the theoretical debate, which at that time was still strongly dominated by the Keynesian view. It is thus appropriate – and necessary – to bring the indications from this Report up to date, in light of the most recent theoretical developments, in order to point out some specific difficulties that characterise the situation of the European Economic and Monetary Union.

A first limitation, already mentioned by the MacDougall Report, concerned the possibility of a direct assumption at the European level of the responsibility for managing the stabilisation policy; this appears to have been overcome with the achievement of Monetary Union, since monetary policy is now a European responsibility. But a second obstacle, regarding the active use of fiscal policy for stabilisation purposes, still exists. In fact, the specific element that characterises the situation in the EU when contrasted with existing federal states is the preponderant weight – with respect to total expenditures – of public expenditures that come from the budgets of the Member States compared to those managed by the Union's budget – which is equal to around 1.0% of European GDP.

It is generally held that, given the present size of the budget and the rules that govern it, the role up to now attributed to the Commission in the management of European-wide stabilisation policy can consist only of promoting the coordination of Member States fiscal policies. These rules determine: the impossibility of closing the budget in deficit (Article 310: "...The revenue and expenditure shown in the budget shall be in bal-

68 R.A. Musgrave, *Theory of Public Finance*, McGraw-Hill, 1959.

69 European Commission, *Report of the Study Group on the Role of Public Finance in European Integration (MacDougall Report)*, Brussels, 1977.

ance…"); the lack of flexibility due to the multi-annual planning (Article 312: "…The multi-annual financial framework shall ensure that Union expenditure develop in an orderly manner and within the limits of its own resources…"); and the need for the Commission to limit additional spending proposals within the limits of its own resources (Article 317: "…The Commission shall implement the budget in cooperation with the Member States […] on its own responsibility within the limits of the appropriations…").

However, coordination of this type must be pursued even if the central government is able to directly manage fiscal policy, at least to the extent necessary to avoid perverse effects with respect to the achievement of the objectives of stabilisation policy. Such coordination must aim at preventing pro-cyclical measures in budgetary policies of local governments, which can reduce expenditure or increase taxes during recessions in order to guarantee a balanced budget – and adopt expansionary policies during growth phases, having a budget surplus available to them. But the provision that is included in the Treaty on the Functioning of the European Union[70] goes further, since it calls for coordination to be the only instrument available for economic policy to deal with symmetrical shocks affecting the Union-wide economy.

Thus, if in this case the burden of stabilisation also falls on the fiscal policy of the Member States, it must be firstly decided whether a limited flexibility in national budgetary choices should be guaranteed. In fact, at the Member State level, given the impossibility of utilising the monetary policy instrument, anti-cyclical variations in the budget balance, with a surplus during expansionary periods and deficits during recessionary ones, should be greater if the responsibility for stabilisation policy falls entirely on the Member States. Secondly, to the extent that the completion of the internal market increases the interdependence of the European economy, there will be a reduction in the willingness of Member States to develop stabilisation policies, since the costs of the policy are borne by their own residents, but the benefits are spread over the entire market. Finally, and most importantly, the effects of a discretionary policy based on the coordination of fiscal measures adopted by Member States tend to occur with a time-lag, to the extent that the stabilising potential of this policy is completely neutralised.

70 Article 175 of TFEU: "Member States shall conduct their economic policies and shall coordinate them in such a way as, in addition, to attain the objectives set out in Article 174".

The coordination of fiscal policies managed by the Member States thus represents a necessary – but not sufficient – condition in order to guarantee the effectiveness of a European stabilisation policy in the face of symmetrical shocks having a significant macroeconomic effect on the whole European economy. In this regard, it should be mentioned that with the previous EMS there was already an asymmetry in the effects of fiscal policy, and thus a deflationary tendency. In fact, when it was necessary to adopt a restrictive fiscal policy – for example, to limit the inflationary effects from an exogenous shock on the cost of inputs – this ran the risk that each Member State would increase taxes or reduce spending, without considering the induced deflationary effects from similar measures taken in other countries. This risk was tied mainly to the determination to achieve the objectives at all costs, without considering the behaviour of other partners. In the case of negative exogenous demand shocks – for example, due to restrictive policies by other countries – the pursuit of expansionary policies will be more difficult because the benefits of the fiscal policy will in any case be partly lost due to the existence of external effects, and the consequent fear of playing the role of the *locomotive*, with the consequent advantages this brings to those partners who behave as *free-riders*.

Coordination can certainly reduce the probability of a deflationary tendency in the management of fiscal policy by Member States of the Monetary Union, but given the time-lags inherent in the political decision-making needed to get this under way, a recessionary effect can occur in any case on output and employment, because of the automatic stabilising effects and the discretionary measures of fiscal policy. On the other hand, it must be emphasised, within the context of problems that arise in reaching an effective political decision, that the weight of the strongest States in defining coordinated measures of fiscal policy is certainly greater – which is normally the case in all confederal political structures. Thus, it appears difficult for the politically and economically weaker Member States to set off down this road with great enthusiasm.

2. The inadequacy of the solutions called for in the Maastricht Treaty

In short, an important limitation of the Maastricht philosophy can be found here. In fact, Article 121 states that "…Member States shall regard their economic policies as a matter of common concern and shall coordinate them within the Council, in accordance with the provisions of Article 120…", which in turn states that "…Member States shall conduct their economic policies with a view to contributing to the achievement of the objectives of the Union…". The Council has to define the general guidelines of the economic policies of the Member States on the basis of the Commission's recommendations. As such, the Commission has no autonomous power to directly manage macroeconomic policy within the Union and can only work towards "…the achievement of the objectives of the Union…" through the coordination of national decisions; and the Treaty did not even foresee an evolution in this policy during the succeeding phases of the EMU. In fact, while the Maastricht Treaty provided for a precise timetable for launching the single currency, Article 310 limited itself to establishing the principle of budget balance at the European level, since "…the revenue and expenditure shown in the budget shall be in balance…". It thus seems clear that there is a need to fill this gap as soon as possible by modifying the provisions of the Treaty regarding the distribution of powers among the Member States and the Commission with respect to the management of economic policy.

From these remarks the conclusion follows that the EMU, in a political context which is destined to develop in a federal direction, must be reconfigured to promote an autonomous stabilisation policy by means of adequate reform in the area of budget policy. This should provide for: a) an increase in the size of the budget, which is moreover unavoidable for allocative reasons alone; b) a change in the budget rules which guarantees compatibility with the objective of monetary stability, but allows at the same time greater elasticity in the management of fiscal policy in order to face negative economic trends; c) the introduction of budgetary instruments which introduce automatic flexibility as regards tax revenue.

Implementation of these reforms presupposes as an essential condition a strengthening of the budgetary authority – made up of the European Parliament and the Council – which also must be given the power to decide on matters concerning the financing of the Union's public expenditure. At present, given the confederal political structure of the Union, restraints on the growth of European public spending are guaranteed by strict budgetary rules, and decisions regarding tax revenues require the unanimous agreement of Member States. But, within a federal political union, which is destined to gradually emerge due to the developments foreseen in the Maastricht Treaty and the evolution of the Monetary Union, it is necessary to ensure that the entire budgetary policy, on both the revenue and expenditure sides, is democratically governed by the joint-decisions of the two branches of the budgetary authority, obviously according to the norms contained in the Treaty, which impose limits on the fiscal policy of the EMU.

Thus, in the area of stabilisation policy it seems useful to re-examine the conclusions of the MacDougall Report, which proposed an increase in the size of the European budget, while at the same time providing it with a certain automatic flexibility. In fact, this solution would have simultaneously solved two problems concerning stabilisation. On one side, an increased budget would allow for sufficient variations in spending – or tax revenues – to counter recessionary or inflationary pressures at the European level. On the other, through the automatic flexibility of the budget it is possible to deal – at least partially – with regional shocks. Here, a member country of the EMU, even if it were no longer able to adjust its monetary policy or exchange rate, could automatically stabilise its economy in case of a recession by paying lower taxes to the European budget and receiving larger transfers (the opposing situation would obviously occur in the event of inflationary pressures).

However, some of the conclusions of the MacDougall Report – which foresaw the need for increasing the size of the budget up to 5-7% of European GDP in order to face the needs of the Monetary Union – even if this increase should be in part compensated for by a parallel reduction in public expenditures at the national level – do not appear realistic today. We now operate in a political context in which all Member States are committed to reducing their deficits, in particular after the launch of the Monetary Union and the approval of the Stability Pact and the Fiscal Compact.

The problem of the optimal size of the budget, to guarantee the effectiveness of stabilisation policy at the European level, features as one of the central themes of a new Report,[71] written by a group of experts on behalf of the European Commission, which updates the conclusions of the 1977 MacDougall Report after the start of the Monetary Union. Regarding the instruments of stabilisation policy in case of symmetrical shocks, the Report's conclusions are entirely conventional. After noting that the most important limits of macroeconomic policy measures aiming at stabilising the economy are connected with the various time-lags which largely compromise its effectiveness, the Report points out that at the European level the only instruments which should be managed by the

71 European Commission, "Stable Money, Sound Finances. Community Public Finance in the Perspective of EMU", in *European Economy*, 1993, No. 53.

EMU are monetary policy and action on the external exchange rate of the euro against the other important world currencies.

Both these policies can have automatic stabilising effects on the overall level of economic activity. In fact, if there is a relatively stable rate of increase in the money supply, interest rates tend to rise during an expansionary phase, thus putting a brake on the increase in demand (and vice-versa during a recession). At the same time, an increase in interest rates causes an inflow of capital from abroad, thereby favouring the appreciation of the euro against other world currencies, thus further slowing down the growth of domestic demand. According to the prevailing opinion among the writers of the Report, given the positive impact on the general economic situation caused by these automatic stabilisation mechanisms, it is not considered necessary to activate an autonomous fiscal policy at the European level, but it is sufficient to promote a coordination of national fiscal policies.

This conclusion could gain partial support, but it has a basic shortcoming. It can be supported because a coordination of national fiscal policies is necessary in any case in order to avoid the perverse effects which could result from conflicting national fiscal policies. However, it is inadequate; all the limitations of time-lags in fiscal policies – which justify a negative conclusion about the possibilities of managing a fiscal policy aimed at stabilisation through discretionary measures – are even more present in the case of a coordination. This – even optimistically assuming an agreement is finally reached – nevertheless require a long period of time to become operative. As a result, the effects of national fiscal policy decisions tend to manifest themselves when general economic circumstances may have already largely changed. The main point is then to see if, besides being necessary, coordination is sufficient for stabilisation purposes, in the absence of other instruments which can be used at the European level.

The fact is that, as far as European stabilisation policy is concerned, the real problem is a political one, and consists in determining the authority that is able in the last instance to make fiscal policy decisions. If there is an effective authority at the European level, endowed with the necessary powers, then a European fiscal stabilisation policy is possible, even if this will have to be achieved partially through the coordination of national fiscal policies. If, however, at the European level there is no autonomous decision-making authority, and coordination can only be carried out through reaching the necessary consensus in the Council, then there is no European policy, but only an inefficient sum of national policies. Moreover, in this case the effects of different national policies can cancel themselves out if the European recommendations are not translated into coherent decisions by each Member State. But even in the most optimistic scenario, where all states carry out European recommendations, the decision-making process in the different countries will nevertheless require a long period of time, and as a result the effects on the economy will occur with a delay that will substantially limit their effectiveness.

Even in this area the experience of the European Union can thus turn out to be innovative, given that the stabilisation policy necessarily requires cooperation at both the European and national government levels. In fact, it is neither necessary, nor opportune, to move from a national policy of stabilisation to one managed exclusively at the European level. In fact, given the relative weights of national budgets and the Union's budget, it can be with reasonable certainty foreseen that the greatest burden for stabilisation policy will remain on the shoulders of Member States' fiscal policy. But there will only be an effective European policy – as opposed to a sum (ineffective) of national policies – if at the European level there are both the financial means to pursue an – even if limited – autonomous stabilisation policy, supported by a real decision-making power regarding the measures to be adopted, and adequate instruments to get the Member States to respect the decisions that have been made regarding coordination of their domestic policies. If this model is realised, then the European Union could in fact represent the first example of a truly federal structure in the management of stabilisation policy, on the basis of the subsidiarity principle sanctioned by Article 5 TEU. But it is clear that the Maastricht Treaty provisions keep us well away from realising this model.

In effect, the solutions identified in the Treaty are limited to a description of the functioning of the multilateral surveillance mechanism. Here, Article 121 establishes the procedure that permits the setting of general guidelines for economic policies of Member States and the Union. If a Member State is found not to be abiding by these guidelines, or risks compromising the correct functioning of the Economic and Monetary Union, "...the Council may, acting by a qualified majority on a recommendation from the Commission, make the necessary recommendations to the Member States concerned...". It is clear that norms of this type are far from recognising an effective decision-making capacity at the Union level. This would allow the precise definition of the necessary fiscal policy measures through the initiative of the Commission and with the consensus of the European Parliament and the Member States – by means of a majority decision in the Council – and would also attribute a real executive power to the Commission to guarantee that the measures decided on become effectively operative, directly through the instruments of the EU budget and indirectly through the cooperation of the Member States.

This conclusion thus appears to be quite important, since it points out that the decisive choice over the macroeconomic stabilisation policy for the European economy is basically political in nature and implies giving the institutions of the European Union a true autonomous ruling power in this area, so that they can make binding decisions for Member States on the overall stance of fiscal policy. In reality, the alternative is not between a European stabilisation policy and the coordination of national fiscal policies, since a European stabilisation policy necessarily includes the coordination of the national fiscal policies among its instruments. Instead the main difference concerns the existence of a real decision-making power at the European level: if this power exists the system is effective; if not, as is still the case in the wake of the Treaty of Maastricht, there is no European policy, but only a sum of national policies, and this solution is completely ineffective.

3. The regional stabilisation policy

A second problem regarding fiscal policy emerges; in a Monetary Union the Member States lose their right to set monetary and exchange rate policies. The theory on optimal currency areas suggests that this problem can be easily solved if there is a sufficiently large federal budget, since the effects of a country-specific shock – or a shock with asymmetrical effects – that hits one member country in the union, are to a significant extent automatically absorbed. The automatic flexibility of the federal budget is thus able to guarantee an effective stabilisation policy at the regional level, despite the loss of two important instruments of economic policy. But if the budget is not sufficiently large, or is not empowered with sufficient flexibility, these automatic mechanisms are not strong enough to avoid the appearance of negative effects from the exogenous shock.

The 1977 MacDougall Report[72] had already proposed a choice in line with the conclusions of the theory on the optimal currency areas, which assumed a federal management of a sufficiently large budget. If such a solution were to be impracticable, the alternative solution would have been the more flexible use of national fiscal policy instruments. But this alternative is now unrealistic, especially when considering the conditions

[72] European Commission, *Report of the Study Group on the Role of Public Finance in European Integration (MacDougall Report)*, Brussels, 1977.

imposed by the Maastricht Treaty and by the Stability Pact and, more recently, by the Fiscal Compact. A careful evaluation of the appropriateness of using alternative instruments that can be implemented at the Union level is thus unavoidable. The objective is to ensure that a country going through a recession is not forced – in order to avoid heavy losses in output and employment – to manage its fiscal policy in such a way as to cause a budget deficit, thus going against the Maastricht prescriptions, or to be obliged to an internal devaluation through a reduction in wages and, consequently, in labour costs in order to improve the competitiveness of domestic production.

On the basis of the available literature and the actual experience of the states with a federal structure, it is generally assumed that the existence of a centralised budget can lead to a significant reduction in the impact of an exogenous shock on a regional economy, a reduction that is larger in states like Germany, where *Länder* can make ample use of the horizontal equalisation mechanisms of the *Finanzausgleich*. It is useful to distinguish between three main channels for absorbing the impact of adverse shocks: a credit channel, since operators may borrow internationally to sustain consumption and investment; a capital market channel, which runs via private investment portfolios; and a public channel which relies on cross-regional fiscal transfers. Cimadomo *et al.* have shown[73] that "...around 60-80% of state-specific shocks is smoothed via the above risk sharing channels in the United States while the corresponding number for the euro area countries has generally been no more than 20% since the start of the EMU...". They then reach the conclusion that "...the euro area would benefit from a central stabilisation function which can support national economies stabilisers in the presence of large economic shocks...".

In general, therefore, these automatic stabilisation mechanisms appear to be adequate to compensate – at least in large part – for the negative effects that could arise for a regional economy hit by an exogenous shock. If the shock is recessionary in nature, then income will be reduced in the region in question, tax revenues – national or federal – will fall, and transfers financed from the central budget will increase. As a result, demand will increase in the region suffering a recession, with positive effects on income and employment levels. Similar effects will occur in the event of inflation caused by excess demand. However, the occurrence of these effects obviously assumes that the size of the central budget allows for significant variations in revenue and spending

---

73 J. Cimadomo, S. Hauptmeier, A.A. Palazzo, A. Popov, "Risk Sharing in the Euro Area", in *Economic Bulletin*, Issue 3, European Central Bank, 2018, pp. 85-98.

levels. Thus, the case is different for the European Union, where the size of the budget barely reaches around 1.0% of GDP and appears, in fact, to be totally insufficient to guarantee the proper functioning of these automatic stabilisation mechanisms, as the MacDougall Report had already pointed out.

However, given the difficulties of immediately increasing the size of the European budget to the necessary extent under the present economic and political situation, it is nevertheless useful to consider the possibility of obtaining comparable results with limited budget resources, if these are specifically allocated to the regional stabilisation policy. In particular, a solution could be imagined involving the creation of a budget fund which can be automatically used to sustain the economy of a Member State if variations in the employment rate in the country in question differ significantly from the Union's average.[74]

Earlier simulation studies supported the idea that if the budget were to set aside 0.2% of European GDP[75] for financing an *ad hoc* mechanism for regional economic stabilisation, this will be enough to guarantee the effectiveness of a stabilisation policy for the economies of the Member States who are faced with an exogenous shock, thereby avoiding the risk of having to turn to internal devaluation as the only practical solution. In particular, the mechanism envisaged in the 1993 Report called for a transfer equal to one percentage point of GDP in favour of the Member States hit by a recessionary shock for every point that the national unemployment rate differs from the Community average, with a ceiling equal to 2% of the GDP of the receiving country. As a result, increases in unemployment above 2% with respect to the Union's average are no longer compensated. In any case, this mechanism seems able to guarantee a stabilisation that is equal on average to 18-19%, quite similar to that which generally exists in states with a federal structure.[76]

---

74 A. Majocchi, M. Rey, "A Special Financial Support Scheme in Economic and Monetary Union: Need and Nature, in The Economics of Community Public Finance", in *European Economy: Reports and Studies*, 1993, No. 5, pp. 457-480.

75 By means of simulation of the functioning of the scheme for the period 1984-1991, it was estimated that the maximum amount of transfer payments effected by the fund on annual basis will be on average equal to 0.23% of the European GDP in the year 1990 (A. Italianer, M. Vanheukelen, "Proposals for Community Stabilization Mechanisms: Some Historical Applications", in *European Economy: Reports and Studies*, 1993, No. 5, pp. 493-510).

76 J. Pisani-Ferry J., A. Italianer, R. Lescure, "Stabilization Properties of Budgetary Systems: A Simulation Analysis", in *European Economy: Reports and Studies*, 1993, No. 5, pp. 511-538.

The implementation of a European regional stabilisation fund – backed by the attribution to the Commission of a true coordinating power regarding the economic policies of the Member States – could promote an effective solution to the problem of stabilisation. In this case it would be easier for Member States in the Union to accept the new conditions imposed by the Stability Pact and the Fiscal Compact, aimed at ensuring monetary stability after the introduction of the euro through the establishment of constraints which are even more rigid than those in the Maastricht Treaty. These constraints would in fact be more manageable in the context of an expanding European economy, if the Member States also benefitted from transfers of a regional stabilisation fund in order to counterweigh the deflationary effects of measures that have necessarily been adopted to improve their budget balance.

4. A European Unemployment Reinsurance Fund (EURF)

Thus far the EU budget has not been designed to support a macroeconomic stabilisation function, but a proposal to overcome this limit was included in the 2015 Five Presidents' Report[77]. While the creation of a euro area fiscal capacity seems to be a reasonable path to be followed in the future, alternatives have been considered for the protection of public investment from economic downturn through, primarily, an unemployment insurance scheme in case of a sudden rise in unemployment.

A European Unemployment Reinsurance Fund (EURF) would provide a common stabilisation function that would bring numerous benefits to the euro area, complementing national budget stabilisers in the case of severe asymmetric shocks, and allowing smoother fiscal policies when monetary policy reaches its limits. This carries a *caveat*: the function should minimise moral hazard and should not lead to permanent transfers or indeed duplicate the role of the EMS. Access should be conditional on compliance with EU fiscal rules and the broader economic surveillance framework.

The EURF would act as a *reinsurance fund* for national unemployment schemes; these represent an important part of the social safety net, but their uptake tends to increase in a downturn, when resources available are constrained by the need to limit fiscal deficits. A genuine EURF is one in which financial transfers from the European fund directly target

77 *The Five Presidents' Report: Completing Europe's Economic and Monetary Union*, Brussels, 22 June 2015.

unemployed individuals, mediated through national benefit schemes. It would require deep harmonisation of national legislation – that is administratively and politically difficult – because citizens should be treated in the same way by the EURF in terms of eligibility requirements, generosity of benefits and the duration and amount of the unemployment benefits.

A mechanism implying financial transfers between different areas belonging to a monetary union may generate a risk of moral hazard, since the government concerned may decide not to implement unpopular policies if it expects to be compensated by increased financial support coming from the upper level of government. To limit this risk the most popular solution is the introduction of a trigger, composed of an indicator and a threshold. In every period in which the indicator exceeds the threshold, transfers are operated towards a particular country. The adoption of a trigger is reasonable in the case of a EURF agreed between countries, not workers, and is more effective when it is related to changes in unemployment rather than levels of unemployment, since every country is likely to be a recipient of transfers at some point in time.

Two important features of the scheme are the size and the financing of the EURF. The size depends on the stabilisation effects that are expected. Naturally, if a trigger is included so that the payment is only disbursed under certain conditions, this makes the scheme much cheaper. The general conclusion reached in the literature usually estimates the cost of an EURF to be between 0.3% and 0.85% of European GDP.[78] As far as the financing of the scheme is concerned, many proposals have been put forward in the literature,[79] but the answer to this question is intrinsically linked to the general problem of a new system of own resources to finance the EU budget.

In its proposal for the next Multiannual Financial Framework,[80] the Commission explained the characteristics of the *European Investment*

---

[78] M. Beblavý, G. Marconi, I. Maselli, *A European Unemployment Benefit Scheme. The rationale and the challenges ahead*, European Commission, Centre for European Policy Studies, Brussels 2015, p. 18. While some proposals envisage a common fund of about 1-2% of euro area GDP (G. Wolff, *A budget for Europe's monetary union*, Bruegel Policy Contribution No. 22, Brussels, 2012), another suggestion for a short-term unemployment insurance at the European level arrives at revenue needs of 0.75% of GDP (S. Dullien, *A euro-area wide unemployment insurance as an automatic stabilizer: who benefits and who pays?*, Paper prepared for the European Commission, DG EMPL, Brussels, 2013).

[79] For an in-depth analysis of the relevant literature: D. Moro, *For a federal European Unemployment Insurance Scheme*, U.E.F. Reflection Paper, Brussels, March 2016.

[80] European Commission, *A Modern Budget for a Union that Protects, Empowers and Defends. The Multiannual Financial Framework for 2021-2027*, COM(2018) 321 final, Brussels, 2 May 2018.

Stabilisation Function, the stabilisation tool intended to be built inside the EU budget – included in a budget line called *Economic and Monetary Union* – that comprises a loan and a grant element. As far as the loan component is considered, the Commission could offer back-to-back loans of up to €30 billion for countries facing asymmetric shocks, which had pursued sound fiscal and economic policies before the shock, this being a good complement to the European Stability Mechanism (ESM) by being unconditional and automatic. But compared to the ESM lending capacity, which is €500 billion, this amount appears as quite negligible. Its main objective should be to maintain investment levels in the event of large asymmetric shocks.

But the Commission also plans a future risk-sharing component, in its proposal to create an EMU stabilisation function, with the idea of building a fund (a Stabilisation Support Fund) with €600 million per year, financed with a share of the seignorage profits from the Eurosystem, that could be used to provide an interest rate subsidy to the countries receiving the loans.[81] In addition, the Commission mentioned that

> the European Investment Stabilisation Function could be later complemented by an insurance mechanism outside of the EU budget, financed by voluntary contributions of Member States to build a rainy-day fund. Even though this could not be based on voluntary contributions, as this would create an adverse selection problem, this potential solution would nevertheless constitute a real answer to stabilisation issues of the euro area.[82]

5. A Rainy-Day Fund

According to recent estimates,[83] only about 20% of exogenous shocks to euro area countries' GDP per capita are smoothed via cross-border risk sharing, while 75% of shocks are smoothed in the United States, mainly by cross-border risk-sharing in capital and credit markets, but

---

81 "We highlight a (modest) possible design not that far from the proposal of the Commission, which might be politically feasible: accumulating all ECB profits in a rainy-day fund, which would be used in a crisis to foster investment throughout the euro area" (G. Claeys, Z. Darvas, *The Commission's proposal for the next MFF: A glass half-full*, Brueghel Blog Post, 25 May 2018).

82 G. Claeys, *New EMU stabilisation tool within the MFF will have minimal impact without deeper budget reform*, Brueghel Blog Post, 9, May 2018.

83 V. Constâncio, *Effectiveness of Monetary Union and the Capital Markets Union*, Speech at the Eurofil Conference, Malta, 6 April 2017.

also by federal transfers. Some steps forward could be achieved by Europe completing the Banking Union and the Capital Markets Union, but private cross-border financial flows are likely to continue to be pro-cyclical and to diminish substantially during crises, as the case was in 2008-09 and 2011-12. Hence, there will be still merit in fiscal risk sharing to help smooth country-specific shocks and to support aggregate euro area demand when monetary policy is constrained.

The IMF underlined in a recent Note[84] that a euro-area fiscal capacity would strengthen countries' ability to smooth country-specific shocks, responding to output fluctuations with countercyclical fiscal policy, but would also be able to cushion area-wide shocks, improving growth and employment scenarios especially when monetary policy has reached its effective lower limit. The main idea underlying this proposal is to create a dedicated macroeconomic stabilisation fund that makes transfers to countries in troubled times, and is financed by regular annual contribution from countries' budgets, to build up assets in good times. This *rainy-day fund* would help countries with limited fiscal head-room avoid a pro-cyclical fiscal tightening in a downturn when revenues fall and cyclical expenditures rise.

The Note analyses the case of a large euro area-wide shock when monetary policy is constrained; they reach the conclusion that for a relatively modest cost – 0.35% of GDP per year – a central fiscal capacity could reduce the negative effects on output by more than 50%. The instrument should be understood as a temporary cushion and the risk that it will generate permanent transfers – that is, the risk of moral hazard – could be avoided if transfers from the fund are conditional on a member's compliance with EU fiscal rules and if the countries pay a premium in good times, based on benefits they receive from the fund in bad times.

Transfers from the fund to national budgets would be triggered automatically by a cyclical indicator that could be the deviation of the unemployment rate from its long-run moving average, since it is harmonised across euro area countries and is more easily observable than other cyclical indicators, such as the output gap or GDP growth. Transfers would be proportional to the deviation: for example, transfers worth 0.5% of the recipient country's GDP could be made for every one point deviation of the unemployment rate, and as a result,

84 N. Arnold, B. Barkbu, E. Ture, H. Wang, J. Yao, *A Central Fiscal Stabilization Capacity for the Euro Area*, IMF Staff Discussion Note, 26 March 2018.

if monetary policy is constrained and interest rates cannot be cut to mitigate the shock, the transfer could reduce the impact of the shock by nearly three-fifths.[85]

The conclusion of the IMF Note is that this is an appropriate time to take the first steps in establishing a Central Fiscal Capacity[86], activating a rainy-day fund. The need to create a stabilisation mechanism has been recognised by both the European Commission and by political leaders, such as the French President and the Italian government.[87] The creation of a rainy-day fund is quite simple from a technical point of view – even if it is politically more difficult to define the size of the contributions and the rate of the transfers – and the risk of moral hazard could be mitigated providing incentives for countries to maintain fiscal discipline, through a revision of fiscal rules that make them less pro-cyclical. But more importantly the expansionary phase of the cycle is the best time to implement this reform, especially if assets should be built up through contributions before activating transfers. Policymakers should seize this favourable, but probably temporary, chance to strengthen euro area resilience to economic euro-area wide and country-specific shocks.

---

[85] N. Arnold *et al.*, p. 19.

[86] O. Fontana, *The Debate on Eurozone Fiscal Capacity*, Centro Studi sul Federalismo, Policy Paper No. 35, Torino, July 2018.

[87] *Initiative pour l'Europe*. Discours d'Emmanuel Macron: *Pour une Europe souveraine, unie, démocratique*, Paris, 26 Septembre 2017; Italian Position Paper, *Reforming the European Monetary Union in a stronger European Union*, Rome, 13 December 2017.

Chapter 5

European policy promoting sustainable growth

1. Weakness of economic policy management in the European Union

The deep crisis that ravaged the world economy after the collapse of Lehman Brothers on September 15, 2008 began in the US, but its main consequences were felt in Europe. Very soon after the Lehman collapse the European banks were affected by the American banks' troubles, forcing European governments to intervene, supporting the banking system with massive injections of public money. At the same time, the banks, facing serious financial difficulties, were forced to impose a credit squeeze on their customers and, in particular, on the production system. Enterprises in financial straits reduced their levels of productive activity with the consequent contraction of families' incomes, bringing about a further impact on demand for consumer goods. At this point, the crisis extended to the real sector and involved, albeit in different ways, all industrialised areas of the world.

Faced with the risk of a global recession, countries reacted immediately, overcoming the tendency to increasingly limit any type of public intervention that had become dominant since the Reagan and Thatcher eras; instead they heavily financed the real economy and, simultaneously, tried to guarantee employment levels through extensive use of social support provisions even if, in Europe in particular, unemployment rose significantly. The reaction to the crisis was stronger and more immediate in the United States than in Europe, where only the European Central Bank – an institution of a federal nature – was in the position to rapidly take the decisions needed to face the greatest economic crisis of the post-war period. The reactions of the EU and Eurozone countries were slower and weaker than those of the US for two self-reinforcing reasons: first of all, the European Union is a structure of a confederal nature as far as interventions in economic policy are concerned. Policy reactions must essentially be based on coordination – slow and inefficient – of decisions taken at the national level;[88] furthermore, as far as fiscal interventions are concerned, decisions must be taken unanimously,[89] leading to further delays with the – inevitable – compromises necessary to reach an agreement.

The second factor that impeded a stronger and quicker reaction results from the fact that in a strictly interdependent economic area, it may be convenient for individual countries to act as free-riders, to wait for other countries to take the initiative, through increased public expenditure or tax reduction, because the positive effects of interventions in other countries quickly spread to the whole area. Consequently, no single European country had an interest in taking on the burden of financing the recovery of the European economy, whose cost would fall on the Member State's citizens, while all of the countries of the economically integrated area would benefit from it. On the other hand, the intervention of the European Union was also constrained by the limited size of the EU budget (around 1% of European GDP). In conclusion, the United States, with its federal government and a budget of a normal size, was quickly able to support the economic recovery with adequate means. In Europe, the economic policy measures needed to face the recession were entrusted to Member States, and were further constrained by the rules of the Stability Pact and the Fiscal Compact regarding

---

88 According to Article 120 of the Treaty on the Functioning of the European Union (TFEU), "...Member States shall conduct their economic policy with a view to contributing to the achievement of the objectives of the Union, as defined in Article 3 of the Treaty on European Union (TEU), and in the context of the broad guidelines referred to in Article 121(2) TFEU. The Member States and the Union shall act in accordance with the principle of an open market economy with free competition, favouring an efficient allocation of resources, and in compliance with the principles set out in Article 119...". In Article 3 TEU, after having stated that "...the Union' aim is to promote peace, its values and the well-being of its peoples...", it is added that "...the Union shall establish an internal market. It shall work for the sustainable development of Europe based on balanced economic growth and social progress, and a high level of protection and improvement of the quality of the environment. It shall promote scientific and technological advance...". Finally, and most important, Article 3(4) TEU states that "...the Union shall establish an Economic and Monetary Union whose currency is the euro...". Then, a Monetary Union is not enough and Europe should proceed towards a full economic union, in view of an *ever closer union among the peoples of Europe...*" (Article 1 TEU).

89 Article 312(2) TFEU states: "...The Council, acting in accordance with a special legislative procedure, shall *unanimously* and after consulting the European Parliament adopt a decision laying down the provisions relating to the system of own resources of the Union..." (Article 311 TFEU). And regarding the Multiannual Financial Framework limiting the development of expenditures "...the Council shall act *unanimously* after obtaining the consent of the European Parliament...".

the extent of public deficits, and had the limited objective of preventing the crisis from turning into a catastrophic recession.

2. The limits of national expansionary policies

Many constraints hinder the process of sustainable growth of the European economy, and the budget problems of many Eurozone countries limit their ability to launch a domestic expansionary policy. As such, the European Union should play a decisive role in helping to strengthen the recovery through a growth policy that will reduce social tensions that have become unbearable in many countries and, thanks to the positive automatic effects on tax revenues of increased GDP, relax the ties that weigh on national budgets. However, the EU's budget resources are limited and, in any case, at the moment some governments seem unwilling to provide the Union with the policy instruments able to support a new phase of rapid and equitable growth in Europe.

The experiences of European countries in the last few years have revealed the limits of the theory of non-Keynesian effects of fiscal policy,[90] and within an important international organisation such as the IMF it has been recently recognised[91] that fiscal multipliers are normally larger than 1 and that fiscal consolidation – that in any case is unavoidable – inevitably brings about deflationary effects.[92] Furthermore, given the interdepend-

---

90 According to the Keynesian theory an increase in public expenditure or a reduction in taxes will provide expansionary effects on GDP. Recently, a new school of thinking has expressed a different view, assuming that a reduction in expenditures or an increase in taxation will increase GDP since people *expect* that a reduced deficit will imply lower tax needs in the future, then more disposable income, and begin immediately to spend more (these are the presumed non-keynesian, expansionary effects of fiscal consolidation). See, for instance: F. Giavazzi, M. Pagano, *Non-keynesian effects of fiscal policy changes: international evidence and the Swedish experience*, NBER WP 5332, National Bureau of Economic Research, November 1995.

91 IMF, *World Economic Outlook*, October 2012, pp. 41-43. See also: O. Blanchard, D. Leigh, *Growth Forecast Errors and Fiscal Multipliers*, IMF Working Paper 13/1, January 2013.

92 In a recent paper it has been underlined that "...the stronger the austerity programme, the deeper the decline in GDP. The estimated equation suggests that on average for every 1% increase in austerity, output declines by 1.4%...". This implies that "...a 1% increase in austerity only leads to a 0.5% improvement in the budget balance. Put another way, in order to improve the budget balance by 1%, an austerity programme of at least 2% is necessary. Given our measure of the fiscal multiplier of 1.4, this also implies a drop in GDP of 2.8%. Thus, the Eurozone austerity programme imposed a very unfavourable trade-off for the periphery countries: in order

ence within the Internal Market, weak growth in one country restricts its imports, and hence exports from other European countries, restraining the economic growth of the entire Eurozone.

There is no national way out of this bottleneck. Expansionary measures are impossible at the level of Member States; many of them are obliged by the Maastricht constraints and the Stability Pact and Fiscal Compact to choose fiscal consolidation as a priority, that is, less expenditures and more taxes. Furthermore, such expansionary measures would in any case be domestically ineffective, since a large part of the effects ensuing from national measures would be lost through increased imports from other European countries. This course of action would result in every country trying to behave like a free-rider, waiting for expansionary measures funded by other Eurozone Member States. Thus, such a stabilisation policy would prove to be sub-optimal.

Therefore, to get out of this impasse, what is needed is to rapidly promote a European plan for sustainable growth. In parallel, given more and more stringent environmental constraints, this initiative should consider the fact the crisis has marked the end of the previous model of growth for the European economy, since it cannot be overcome with a policy exclusively aiming to support the demand for consumer goods that uses a large amount of natural resources.

3. A policy promoting investments and production of public goods

Many steps have been taken towards effective governance of the Eurozone area for the sake of guaranteeing financial stability, with the signature of the Treaty on Stability, Coordination and Governance (the Fiscal Compact) in March 2012, the Six Pack in December 2011, and

---

to improve their government budget balance by 1% a sacrifice of 2.8% of GDP was necessary…". The political conclusion follows that "…the imposition of austerity programmes in the Eurozone has fallen victim to the fallacy of composition. What works for one nation fails to work when every nation applies the same policies (…). When all countries try to save more at the same time, each country's attempt to do so makes it harder for the others to achieve their objectives…". Then, "…it is high time that the Commission takes up its role of defending the interests of the debtor nations with the same vigour that it defends the interests of the creditors…". See: P. De Grauwe, Y. Ji, *The Legacy of Austerity in the Eurozone*, CEPS Commentary, 4 October 2014.

the Two Pack's entry into force in May 2013.[93] Furthermore, with the approval of these rules it is clear that there is now a general consensus that each country is obliged to comply with the duty to pay back its own debt accumulated in the past. Measures are now in place to ensure that financial stability will be pursued by each Member State within the Eurozone under stringent European control. But fiscal consolidation will be difficult to achieve if a new phase of strong economic growth of the European economy is not rapidly forthcoming.

Structural reforms are urgently needed and unavoidable in indebted countries, to improve productivity and to increase competitiveness, but the positive results of these reforms will be achieved only in the medium and long term. Therefore, in order to strengthen the recovery process, it is necessary to initiate a new phase of growth and to promote an increase in employment by linking a policy of fiscal consolidation in each Member State with the immediate creation within the European budget of a sufficiently large fund, targeted to promoting growth and employment,[94] since growth must be supported by a European initiative.

Huge investments from both the public and private sectors are needed to meet infrastructure challenges. The fund could immediately start to finance these projects, while promoting a policy to improve in the medium term the competitiveness of the European economy through investments in higher education, research, and technological innovation. A smaller part of the fund's capacity could be used to support structural reforms in Member States that enter into arrangements of a contractual nature with EU institutions through limited, temporary, flexible, and targeted financial incentives – the Convergence and Competitiveness Instrument suggested by the Commission.[95]

A traditional policy based only on the support of demand for consumption is, in the current conditions, largely inadequate. A new phase of growth in the European economy should be opened by promoting a sustainable development model.[96] Public investments should become

---

93 European Commission, *Six-pack? Two-pack? Fiscal compact? A short guide to the new EU fiscal governance*, available at http://ec.europa.eu/economy_finance/articles/governance/2012-03-14_six_pack_en.htm.

94 A. Majocchi, *A European Fund for Growth and Employment: A First Step Toward a Eurozone Budget*, German Marshall Fund Policy Brief, June 2014.

95 European Commission, *A blueprint for a deep and genuine Economic and Monetary Union. Launching a European debate*, COM(2012) 777 final, Brussels, 28 November 2012.

96 The social dimension should be included in this model. This implies in particular the adoption of measures targeted to support employment, especially of young people,

the driver of growth, with a positive short-run impact on demand, but also on long-run growth through an increase in potential output. The main declared goal of the fund should be the improvement of European citizens' quality of life, and raising the productivity of European firms, through increased spending on cutting-edge research and higher education, strengthening the material and immaterial infrastructure network, promoting energy efficiency and the use of renewable energy sources, supporting a soft mobility that does not worsen environmental conditions, guaranteeing conservation of cultural and natural assets, and favouring urban renewal.

In the United States, the growth of the economy largely depends on expansionary monetary policy measures, mainly targeted at supporting an expansion of demand in consumption and the building industry. This type of policy measure is inconceivable in Europe, where the solution to the main problem centres on increasing productivity to face the competitiveness challenge within the global economy and on favouring a reduction in the rate of unemployment, whereas for environmental purposes the amount of land available – a truly scarce resource – must be protected against excessive use. It is true that Europe suffers from a lack of consumption demand, but this problem should be addressed through effective redistribution measures in favour of the lower income classes, and not with credit measures.[97]

With the approval of the Fiscal Compact the European countries have made an innovative choice compared to its past experiences: growth will no longer depend on the creation of new debt. In the meantime, it has become generally recognised that economic development should be compatible with environmental conservation. Current expenditures should

---

but also the provision of adequate skills for workers that have lost employment due to technological changes and the strengthening of the welfare structure in face of the challenges raised by an ageing population. In this area a new starting point could be represented by the jointly approval, at the Social Summit held in Gothenburg on 17 November 2017, of the European Pillar of Social Rights by the European Parliament, the Council and the European Commission. A first step in this direction is represented by L. Fransen, G. del Bufalo, E. Reviglio, *Boosting Investments in social infrastructure in Europe*, Report of the High-level Task Force on investing in Social Infrastructure in Europe chaired by R. Prodi and C. Sautter, Discussion Paper 074, Brussels, 23 January 2018.

97 This issue has been recently restored in the political debate, with many important contributions: T. Piketty, *Capital in the Twenty-First Century*, Harvard Univ. Press, 2014; J.E. Stiglitz, *The price of inequality. How today's divided society endangers our future*, W.W. Norton, 2012; A.B. Atkinson, *Inequality. What can be done?*, Harvard Univ. Press, 2015.

be funded with tax resources, while the issuance of bonds should be targeted only at financing investments, and not the current account. To be consistent with this choice, the fund created within the European budget should devote its resources to the financing of material investment, the production of human capital or of collective goods in order to support sustainable development, increased productivity and, consequently, of the competitiveness of the European economy.

In past years Europe has not contributed substantially to countering the crisis, but has paid a huge cost for it. In this way it atones for its inability to take part in the governance of the process of globalisation, lacking the real power to play an active role in the establishment of a new world equilibrium. Equally, the European Union is unable to effectively face the current difficulties, lacking real power to govern the economy. But it should also be emphasised that a phase of growth in the European economy – that characterised the second half of the previous century – has now definitively ended. The main factor determining growth rate was technological progress through the importation of the best technologies from the most advanced foreign countries in order to raise productivity and to increase the standard of living of European people. But the European economy has now reached the technological limit and is unable to restart high rates of growth through the importation of technologies from abroad. For a new phase of growth to be stimulated, Europe must exploit its own resources and, in particular, must promote an autonomous capacity of innovation in order to enhance the productivity and competitiveness of its industrial system on the global market.

At the global level the pattern of growth followed in the past is now unsustainable, from all points of view. The planet's environment is unable to support the enormous increases of pressure on natural resources. From the point of view of equality, it seems unacceptable that more than one billion human beings living in the poorest countries be excluded from a reasonable standard of living. Finally, while the availability of consumer goods has been continuously increasing, even in affluent societies many essential needs are not adequately satisfied. Hence, policy measures to support demand for consumption are not an effective way out from the current crisis; a new plan for the promotion of sustainable development – from an economic, social and environmental point of view – must be carried out as soon as possible.

The driver of this new pattern of growth should be public investments targeted not only at building up the most needed material infrastructures, but also to support higher education and research and development expenditures so that technological innovation can be promoted and upheld. A policy based on investment promotion will have either short-run effects on demand and employment, with a positive impact on GDP growth, or long-run effects on supply, enhancing potential income and improving the competitiveness of the European economic system. The achievement of these goals is essential so that the financial sustainability of the welfare system prevailing in Europe can also be guaranteed for future generations.

However, some Member States of the European Union are held in a more and more vicelike grip: from one side, they are obliged to adopt measures, highly costly and immediately effective, to avoid the risk of failure of the weakest part of their industrial and financial sectors; from the other, they must support workers having lost their jobs and, more generally, low-income people hit heavily by the crisis of the last few years. Furthermore, these measures must be adopted when public finances have been endogenously damaged by falls in income, and are constrained by the need to comply with the limits of the Maastricht Treaty in order to avoid market sanctions through an enlarged spread on bonds emissions.

A policy promoting an accelerated rate of growth should be adopted at the European level in order to start a process of sustainable development within Europe. This policy should be targeted at strengthening the European economic and social model through the implementation of a plan providing the funding of expenditure projects in different areas:

- investments for completing the European network in the fields of transport, energy and telecommunications,
- research and development expenditure and promotion of higher education, to strengthen the competitiveness of European production,
- public and private investments in advanced technologies and support to European champions in new leading industrial sectors,
- promotion of renewable energy sources aiming at a zero-carbon economy,
- projects improving the quality of life for European citizens (water and air quality, sustainable mobility, urban renewal, efficient personal services, especially for vulnerable people), and
- investments to promote conservation and to enlarge utilisation of cultural goods and natural resources.

4. The Juncker Plan: a turning point, but not enough

A change of attitude has recently emerged on policy choices to be adopted for promoting European growth. Supply side reforms are still considered unavoidable, but nevertheless insufficient. While the goals of fiscal consolidation and labour market reform are recognised as important in the medium term, what appears to be urgently needed is a demand-side policy to counter weak domestic demand for consumption and to encourage investment. Up to now, monetary policy has been the only instrument available to provide the necessary liquidity to the market, and the decision of the European Central Bank, to make a monthly purchase through the secondary market (that will be gradually restricted in the last trimester of 2018 to €15 billion and will be brought to a close at the end of this year) of euro-denominated investment-grade securities issued by euro area governments and agencies and European institutions, has really proved the important role played by the only institution of a federal nature tasked with economic policy within the euro area.[98]

The adoption of the Juncker Plan represented a turning point, showing that the prevailing point of view in the Commission was that a fiscal shock for supporting investment demand was needed to complement the efforts of the ECB. According to this plan, the Commission concluded an agreement with the European Investment Bank (EIB) on the establishment of a European Fund for Strategic Investments (EFSI), which would benefit from a guarantee of up to €16 billion by the EU and €5 billion by the EIB in order to conduct its financing and investment operations. The financial resources required would be found by reducing other appropriations within the existing European budget. This does not seem the best path to follow. There are two main flaws in the plan: firstly, there is no additional public money on the table and, secondly, there is a problem of governance since the choice of investments and the distribution of benefits among Member States is not a technical issue, but requires a political choice that cannot be assigned to the EIB.

An effective growth plan implies the collection of new taxes and, guaranteed by these funds, eurobonds could be emitted in sufficient measure to finance investments targeted at the completion of the infrastructure network in Europe. In the meantime, tax revenues could finance the provision of European public goods (*in primis*, expenditures on R&D and the promotion of higher education), in order to support structural change in

---

98 R. Castaldi, *La BCE: la forza di un'istituzione federale*, Centro Studi sul Federalismo, Torino, Commento No. 77, 14 marzo 2016.

the European economy, strengthening the competitiveness of European firms and improving the quality of life of European citizens. The decisive challenge is to provide *appropriate fiscal capacity* to the Union, as proposed in a previous Blueprint by the European Commission:[99] defining the resources that can be collected from taxpayers, allocating part of these resources within the budget to a line specifically appointed to the Eurozone countries, and deciding at the same time to transfer responsibility for directly managing the growth plan to the Commission, under the control of the European Parliament.

According to the Juncker Plan the EFSI should be set up within the EIB as a dedicated trust fund. But if new own resources are allocated to financing a budget line within the Union budget, the creation of a Minister of Economy and Finance within the Commission should be envisaged to manage expenditure policy.[100] However, given the harshness of the economic downturn during the crisis that hit Europe, the huge ensuing social costs, and the time period required for the Juncker Plan to extensively deploy its positive effects on the European economy, transitory and extraordinary measures should be immediately implemented to increase the financial capacity of the EFSI, using all the legal instruments that are now available. Additional financial contributions could be obtained from Member States, and these could also co-finance individual projects financed by the EFSI, through its banking system. This co-financing would benefit from the *investment clause* if the GDP growth of a Member State is negative or GDP remained well below its potential. According to the new flexibility rules proposed by the Commission,[101] these payments will not negatively affect compliance with the deficit or debt rules established by the Stability and Growth Pact.

Furthermore, it must be remembered that 12% of the ECB's liquidity injection, via Quantitative Easing, can be used to purchase securities on the secondary market issued by European Community institutions or by European agencies (such as the EIB or ESM), and then ultimately to purchase bonds from the EIB or from the European Fund for Strategic Investments (EFSI) created by the Juncker Plan. In this context, a recent

99 *Towards a genuine Economic and Monetary Union*, Report by the President of the European Council, Brussels, 5 December 2012.

100 A. Majocchi, *Un piano per l'Europa. Sviluppo sostenibile e occupazione*, Il Mulino, Bologna, 2015, pp. 164-169.

101 European Commission, *Making the best use of the flexibility within the existing rules of the stability and growth pact*, COM(2015) 012 final, Brussels, 10 February 2015.

paper[102] examined the state of play of the Juncker Plan and put forward a proposal to raise this 12% to at least 20% (a percentage corresponding to that part of the ECB's liquidity injections not guaranteed by the national central banks).

5. New resources for funding the Juncker Plan

Since the outbreak of the crisis, public and private investment has been declining. Different estimates quantify the current gap in a range between €190 billion for the Eurozone and €300 billion for the EU as a whole per year,[103] and current initiatives can contribute to bringing current investment levels up to their full potential. During the whole period up to February 2018, EFSI is expected to trigger €264.3 billion in investments – meeting 84% of the original €315 billion target – with 366 infrastructure and innovation projects approved and 589,000 SMEs expected to benefit. The main beneficiaries are Italy, France, Germany and the United Kingdom. From these data it could be noted that "… the size of the mobilized resources is not enough to compensate the EZ investment gap. Hence a more systemic way to mobilize resources has to be introduced…".[104]

The proposal in a nutshell is to substantially increase the amount of QE asset purchases by the ECB from the EIB in order to finance supranational investments. The EIB would issue new bonds (*Investments Bonds*) and sell them on the markets. At present, the EIB has issued additional bonds to the extent of €60 billion, three times the guarantee of the EFSI (€21 billion), while the remainder (up to €315 billion) has been collected through private financing. The *internal multiplier* has to be increased. The ECB should be ready to buy *Investment Bonds* on the secondary market within the framework of a renewed QE through an increase of base money on the liabilities side of ECB's balance sheet. More funds would thus be made available for the EFSI, which could

---

[102] O. Fontana, S. Vannuccini, *Conventional Direction to Unconventional Measures: Using Quantitative Easing to Shape Eurozone Fiscal Capacity*, Centro Studi sul Federalismo Research Paper, Turin, May 2016. In the same perspective a previous contribution is: A. Watt, *Quantitative easing with bite: a proposal for conditional overt monetary financing of public investment*, IMK WP 148, March 2015.

[103] E. Rubio, D. Rinaldi, T. Pellerin-Carlin, *Investment in Europe: making the best of the Juncker Plan. With case studies on digital infrastructure and energy efficiency*, Notre Europe Studies and Report, No. 109, March 2016.

[104] O. Fontana, S. Vannuccini, *ibidem*, p. 16.

expand grants to the States according to some equity criteria. In the proposal it is explicitly stated that Member States will continue to be responsible for their level of earlier debt and will bear the cost of debt servicing on grants received.

In order to be of significant magnitude, while remaining compatible with existing rules, the purchasing of EIB bonds which are part of the investment program should be increased within the 20% risk-sharing regime of the Juncker Plan, given the amount of monthly asset purchases, through a corresponding decrease in the share of other European institutions' securities and government and agencies bodies. In a second phase the EFSI could become part of a Euro Treasury under the control of the European Parliament, as proposed by Bibow,[105] the French and German Governors of their respective Central Banks,[106] and an Italian Minister of Economy and Finance.[107]

6. The External Investment Plan

With all its limitations, it must be recognised that the Juncker Plan represents a turning point, showing for the first time that within the Commission the point of view has prevailed that a fiscal boost towards supporting investment demand is needed to complement the efforts of the ECB. This European Investment Plan, which aims to increase the efficiency of the European economy, represents a significant instrument to accelerate the growth rate of European production. But other urgent problems are pending, and especially the issues of external security and migration. In an important contribution to shaping an EU strategy on migration,[108] the previous Italian government has underscored that the goal for all the existing initiatives in the field of external action should be to develop an active strategy, focusing first and foremost on the African countries of origin and transit of migrants, providing investment projects of high social and infrastructural impact, identified together with the African partner countries.

---

105 J. Bibow, *Making the Euro Viable: The Euro Treasury Plan*, Levy Institute WP, No. 84, July 2015.

106 J. Weidman, F. Villeroy de Galhau, *L'Europe à la croisée des chemins*, Banque de France, February 2016.

107 P.C. Padoan, *Il faut un ministre unique des Finances de la zone euro*, Le Figaro, 30 Mars 2016.

108 Italian Non-Paper, *Migration Compact. Contribution to an EU-Strategy for External Action on Migration*, Presidenza del Consiglio, Roma, 15 April 2016.

In the same perspective, on 14 September 2016 the European Commission proposed an ambitious External Investment Plan,[109] to support investment in the partner countries in Africa (and the European Neighbourhood) to promote a new model for participation by the private sector and help achieve the Sustainable Development Goals, adopted by the United Nations on September 2015. This external action is conceived in the same spirit as the Juncker Plan through the creation of a new European Fund for Sustainable Development (EFSD), which is expected to trigger additional public and private investment volumes, providing partial guarantees to intermediary financing institutions that will, in turn, provide support via loans, guarantees, equity or similar products, to end beneficiaries. In this way the EFSD could mobilise total investments up to €44 billion, based on a €3.35 billion contribution from the EU budget and the European Development Fund. If Member States fully match the European contribution, this action could mobilise more than €88 billion in additional investment.

In fact, this action could represent a crucial instrument for controlling the flow of migrants moving from African countries to Europe, particularly in the case of economic migrants coming mainly from Sub-Saharan countries where the global economic crisis has resulted in a further deterioration of living conditions. Between 2010 and 2015, African GDP grew 3.3% a year, a sharp decline from the 5.4% average annual growth rate achieved between 2000 and 2010. But these global figures misrepresent the real situation since the overall slowdown in Africa's growth is largely dependent on what happens in the North African countries, caught up in the turmoil of the Arab Spring, and in the oil exporting countries, affected by a sharp drop in oil prices.

In the Arab Spring countries (Egypt, Libya and Tunisia, together representing 18% of total African GDP) the real annual growth rate in 2015 was zero (compared to 4.8% between 2000 and 2010); in the oil exporting countries (Algeria, Angola, Chad, Democratic Republic of Congo, Equatorial Guinea, Gabon Nigeria and Sudan, representing 40% of African GDP) it was 4% (7.3% between 2000 and 2010), while in the rest of Africa (42% of African GDP) the growth rate was higher in 2015, at 4.4% (4.1% between 2000 and 2010).

Despite this slowdown in growth rates in recent years, the overall outlook remains promising since the rate of growth in real terms of African

109 European Commission, *Strengthening European Investments for jobs and growth: Towards a second phase of the European Fund for Strategic Investments and a new European External Investment Plan*, COM(2016) 581 final, 14 September 2016.

GDP has more than doubled, from 2% between 1980 and 1990 to 5% between 2001 and 2014, and is still expanding faster than the world average (it was 3.7% in 2016, but is expected to reach 4.5% in 2017). Furthermore, there are certain factors that will contribute largely to increasing the rate of economic growth in African countries.[110]

The first is rapid urbanisation, strongly correlated to the rate of real GDP growth, as productivity in cities is more than double that in the countryside. Africa has a large and young workforce, an important asset in an ageing world. An expanding working-age population is generally associated with strong rates of GDP growth. The employment of this workforce depends largely on the ability of African countries to fully exploit the huge potential from accelerating technological change. This in turn is strictly linked to a massive increase in expenditures targeted on creating human capital. Furthermore, Africa contains 60% of the world's unutilised, but potentially available, agricultural land, as well as the world's largest reserves of mineral resources.

The exploitation of this growth potential is mainly hampered by the lack of availability of much needed investments in infrastructure. For instance, 600 million Africans are without any electricity or lighting; the African Union has agreed to create a Continent-wide Agency for electrification, which has elaborated a plan to reach the goal of 100% electrification in 10 years. The implementation of this plan will require financial aid from the EU of $5 billion yearly for ten years, and this will provide the leverage for releasing private funds of up to $250 billion, needed to realise the plan for electrification.

Three hundred million Africans are without access to clean water and only 5% of available arable land is properly irrigated. But beneath the dry African soil there are reserves full of underground water: according to recent figures collected by the British Geological Survey and University College London,[111] the water reserves are 100 times greater than the volume of water available above ground. The supply of water could be further increased through the use of the new, technologically advanced, desalination plants. This opportunity could be exploited if the electricity required is provided through major investments in solar energy production.

Investments in water and energy supply and production of human capital are the first requirements for an effective African growth plan,

---

110 A. Majocchi, *Migration Compact and African Growth*, Centre for Studies on Federalism. Turin, Comment No. 92, 7 November 2016.

111 A.M. MacDonald, H.C. Bonsor, B.E. Ó Dochartaig, R.G. Taylor, "Quantitative Maps of Groundwater Resources in Africa", in *Environmental Resource Letters*, 7, 2012.

which the European Fund for Sustainable Development should support to effectively deal with the challenge of managing the increasing flow of migrants moving toward European coasts. But this plan has to comply with political requirements as well. The first is the establishment of political stability and security conditions in those African countries from which the migration flows originate, and this should be a priority task in the perspective opened by the new EU Global Strategy[112] conceived by Federica Mogherini, the High Representative of the Union for Foreign Affairs and Security Policy. But many steps forward must be achieved to allow the EU to play a crucial role in the field of foreign and security policy.

To be successful, the growth plan should be designed and implemented at the regional level, supported by an institutional agreement, much like the Marshall Plan in Europe. In his famous speech at Harvard University on 5 June 1947, General Marshall proposed the granting of economic and financial assistance to all countries of Europe, subject to closer European cooperation. On 16 April 1948 in Paris 16 European countries signed a Convention to establish the Organisation for European Economic Cooperation. Launching his plan for European recovery after World War II, Marshall said: "…it would be neither fitting nor efficacious for the American government to undertake to draw up unilaterally a program designed to place Europe on its feet economically. This is a business of the Europeans. The initiative must come from Europe and the program should be a joint one…".[113] This lesson should now be remembered by the EU, when promoting the External Investment Plan. European financial aid is unavoidable, but the initiative should remain in the hands of the African countries concerned.

A first step in this direction has been already put in place. The African Continental Free Trade Area Agreement (AfCFTA), recently signed in Kigali by 44 States,[114] commits the signatories to the removal of import custom duties and tariff barriers on 90% of trade among African countries. At the same time, 27 countries have signed a second Protocol promoting free movement of people across their borders. AfCFTA concerns 1.2 billion people and an aggregate GDP at the continental level reaching about

---

[112] European Commission, *Shared Vision, Common Action: A Stronger Europe. A Global Strategy for the European Union's Foreign and Security Policy*, Brussels, June 2016.

[113] The original text of Marshall speech available at https://library.harvard.edu/sites/default/files/1947_marshall.pdf.

[114] Actually, some countries – Burundi, Uganda, Benin, Namibia, Eritrea, Sierra Leone and, most of all, Nigeria and South Africa, the two economic giants of the continent – have not signed the agreement.

two thousand billion dollars. But in 2018 there are 420 million persons living below the threshold of poverty, and climate changes are impairing agricultural production through widespread drought. Every year the number of young Africans trying to find a job on the labour market amounts to 10-12 million. The goal of the AfCFTA – that will be applied when at least 22 countries ratify the text, in a time frame that has been limited to 18 months – is to increase the level of exchanges taking place between countries of the Continent up to 52%.

In the near future it will be possible to freely exchange goods in Africa without custom barriers and to move without border controls from one country to another. The European Union has certainly been the model for this development. Now the time is ripe for Europe to urgently implement the External Investment Plan to help African countries to improve their economic conditions, putting in place a Marshall Plan for Africa – already envisaged by Altiero Spinelli in 1978[115] – with the goal of not only promoting continental economic development, but also favouring the creation of an open market for the export of European goods, while representing at the same time the first effective step in the control of the flow of migrants towards European countries.

The solution of the problem of migrants depends in the first place on the capacity of African countries, from where in large measure the migrants originate, to promote a growth process able to guarantee jobs and reasonable incomes, especially for younger generations. But the main responsibility falls on European shoulders; it should provide the resources for financing investments and human capital formation, while ensuring at the same time political stability and security to the countries concerned by the African growth plan.

115 A. Spinelli, *PCI, che fare? Riflessioni su strategia e obiettivi della sinistra*, Torino, Einaudi, 1978.

Part II

New resources for the EU budget

Chapter 6

New own resources for the EU budget

1. Double dividend and fiscal reform

The urgency of an in-depth reform of the financing structure of the European budget has emerged recently in the political debate, for a number of concurrent reasons. In the political agenda there is a continuous call concerning the resources needed to face the new tasks that, in growing measure, should be assigned to the Union. In particular, Europe is obliged to cope with difficult security problems, not least following the disengagement of the United States. These concern: the protection that in the past has been guaranteed for the defence of the European territories; the many conflicts in nearby countries or in zones that are of a strategic interest for Europe – mainly in the Mediterranean area or in the Middle East; and the fight against terrorism and the control of migration. But, at the same time, more expenditure is needed as well to promote the competitiveness of the European economy in a globalised world and to support social stability following the dramatic changes in the labour market due to the technological revolution.

Confronted with these increased expenditure needs the European institutions and the Member States' governments are more and more conscious of not only the excessively constraining quantitative limits – around 1% of European GDP – derived from the restricted size of the budget, but also of the inadequacy of the financing structure inherited from the past, that appears increasingly unable to face efficiently, and equitably, the new requirements and to adapt to the structural changes that have taken place in recent years. It thus seems imperative to reach a wide agreement involving firstly political and social forces, but also acceptable to public opinion, on the choices to be pursued in order to achieve a renewal of the structure of public finance within the European Union.

Many contributions to this debate have been made recently, but in the past an innovative suggestion regarding the reform of the public finance structure within the Union had already been foreseen in the Delors' White Paper,[116] where the idea was put forward that energy and the carbon content of fossil fuels should be taxed, so that energy saving and fuel switching could be achieved, and the revenue could be used to cut social security contributions, in order to exploit a double dividend, at least in the weak version.[117] This means that a double goal could be pursued: from one side, to diminish pollution and in particular to curb carbon dioxide emissions and, at the same time, to promote a new phase of sustainable growth of the European economy. This would bring an increase in production and a slowdown of unemployment, since firms and families enjoy, following cuts in social contributions, higher after-tax incomes – while keeping the same level of nominal wages – and external competitiveness of the productive system is improved.

The model that inspired this proposal was the fiscal reform introduced in Sweden during the beginning of the 1990s. The goal of the Swedish government was to efficiently face a double problem: the risk of climate changes linked to growing emissions of carbon dioxide and the rise of unemployment due to weak effective demand. But, at the same time, the crisis of the progressive income tax structure was one of the motivations for this reform, since in it was only workers who were particularly hit by income tax, while capital income and profits were burdened only by a proportional rate.

2. Other factors impacting on the fiscal structure

The need to profoundly alter the structure of European expenditure financing has been strengthened by two important factors that have been operating at the global level: globalisation and the technological revolution. Globalisation has increased the difficulty of taxing capital income, since capital is extremely volatile, while aggressive fiscal avoidance by multinational firms, in particular digital firms, and damaging fiscal competition between different fiscal systems contributes to a transfer of the tax base of these firms to countries where the level of

---

116 European Commission, *Growth, Competitiveness, Employment. The Challenges and Ways Forward into the 21st Century*, White Paper, COM(93) 700, Brussels, 5 December 1993.

117 A.L. Bovenberg, "Green Tax Reforms and the Double Dividend: An Updated Reader's Guide", in *International Tax and Public Finance*, 1999, No. 6, 3, 421-443; L.H. Goulder, "Environmental Taxation and the 'Double Dividend': A Reader's Guide", in *International Tax and Public Finance*, 1995, 2, 2, pp. 157-183.

taxation is lower. Consequently, to keep the same amount of public expenditure, the tax burden on labour incomes must increase significantly, mainly on wages.

Equally, the technological revolution favours the replacement of labour by machines;[118] the employment of labour in the industrial sector is continuously diminishing and only highly specialised labour is able to find employment, either in the industrial sector or, mainly, in the sector of new services, whose share of GDP is progressively increasing. Income tax receipts, largely guaranteed by withholding tax on wages, are diminishing and this reduction is compensated with difficulty by an increase of tax revenue flowing from industrial and self-employment incomes, or from the services sector.

In Europe, besides these factors that weigh heavily on the structure of fiscal systems in industrialised countries all over the world, new tensions emerged after the explosion of the economic crisis, originating in the United States, but more seriously impacting the European countries. While in the United States the federal government had the power to intervene immediately and with a large amount of funds, firstly to save the financial sector and, then, to support production levels, in Europe the recovery has been slower and more complex. Practically, the task of supporting economic recovery had been put in the hands of the European Central Bank, the only federal institution of the Monetary Union. However, coordinated fiscal policy, whose effectiveness would had been greater if managed by the European authorities,[119] was blocked by the rules of the Treaty requiring unanimity for taking decisions at this level, and from the lack of the political will to complete the Fiscal Union. On the other side, the difficult conditions of public finance in many countries of the euro area – following increased expenditures and lower tax revenues due to the economic downturn – have justified the political choice of strengthening the constraints of the Stability Pact and approving the more stringent rules of the Fiscal Compact, further limiting the possibility of managing an expansionary fiscal policy at the national level.

---

118 45% of jobs in the UK, 50% in France, 55% in Greece and 60% in Italy are considered at risk of computerization (G. Ottaviano, *I nuovi dilemmi dei Governatori*, Il Sole 24Ore, 25 August 2017).

119 "At the zero lower bound of nominal interest rates, the domestic GDP effect of a fiscal expansion, *e.g.* an increase in government consumption, is around 40% to 50% higher when implemented jointly in all euro area countries as compared when a country acts alone" (European Fiscal Board, *Assessment of the prospective fiscal stance appropriate for the euro area*, 20 June 2017, p. 6, note 3).

An in-depth rethinking of the goals and structure of the European budget is thus unavoidable to face these changes. According to classic theory going back to Musgrave,[120] the budget has three main functions: allocation of resources between private and public goods, stabilisation and growth of the economy and income redistribution. In turn, the theory of fiscal federalism proposed by Oates[121] – developing on Musgrave's model – is largely different from that achieved in Europe in terms of the distribution between the European and the national levels of the different public functions through the budget. As far as stabilisation is concerned, this remains widely a national task, while only the ruling of monetary policy has been attributed to a European institution (the ECB); the production of European public goods is extremely restrained and income redistribution is constrained within the limits of Member States, while the Union can intervene only to promote territorial redistribution in view of restoring cohesion among countries with different income levels. But today the role of these functions is rapidly changing and, consequently, the instruments to be utilised must change as well.

3. A new structure for the fiscal system

The choice of a renewed structure for the financing of the Union's budget is further complicated by the transition phase that the European economy is going through, that influences to a large degree the selection of new fiscal resources. In general terms, it should be remembered that the main elements of the structure of the fiscal systems in the different countries of the European Union, which collected globally in 2016 40% of GDP, are the following: a) income taxation, that provides a revenue equal to 13.0% of GDP, mainly through the withholding tax on labour incomes; b) consumption taxes, whose receipts equal 13.6% of GDP, mainly through the revenue of VAT and excises; c) social contributions, that represent 13.3% of GDP.[122]

But, firstly, technological developments, and the corresponding changes to the structure of the European economy to which they have given rise, necessarily imply that as far as taxation structure is concerned, important innovations are also needed in the design of the main taxa-

---

120 R.A. Musgrave, *The Theory of Public Finance, A Study in Public Economy*, New York, McGraw-Hill, 1959.

121 W.E. Oates, *Fiscal Federalism*, Harcourt, Brace, Jovanovich, 1972.

122 Eurostat, *Tax revenue statistics*, 6 December 2017.

tion instruments. The first factor of change that must be recognised is the progressive reduction of employment in the industrial sector, whose share of total employment fell from 20.7% in 1996 to 15.3% in 2016.[123] This change will progressively impact on not only the revenue flowing from personal income taxation – since this depends largely from the withholding tax collected by firms on the wages of the workers – but also on social contributions paid by firms, calculated on total payroll.

The second factor is represented by the environmental problem. Due to the globalisation process, the world has reached the limits of available natural resources. Ecological equilibrium had been possible in the past, even if with difficulty, since a large part of world population accepted, given their existing level of poverty, a consumption model that was more restrained in comparison to the opulent consumption of rich countries. But, following the delocalisation of production processes, made economically convenient by technological developments, in particular with regard to information, communication and transport technologies, the growth rate of industrially emerging countries has been rapidly accelerating and, in parallel, pressure on natural resources has increased together with a rising level of consumption. The main effect of this increased pressure manifests itself through the rise in prices of raw materials, but in a still larger measure through excessive pollution both at the local and the global level. This should be countered by measures requiring a large amount of money if a high quality of life is to be maintained, while simultaneously ensuring an adequate supply of natural resources for future generations.

The third factor to be considered concerns the enormous development of the financial sector in comparison with the real economy. This development has been largely determined by the process of liberalisation of capital movements and, particularly, by the deregulation of financial markets, that took place during the Reagan Presidency in the United States and under the Thatcher government in the UK. The Glass-Steagall Act, introduced in the United States in 1993 to control financial speculation, was repealed in practice with the introduction in 1999 of the Gramm-Leach-Bliley Act, which abolished the clear separation between investment and commercial banking. This decision contributed significantly to the creation of the financial bubble that, once burst, caused the beginning of the crisis with the failure of Lehman Brothers on 15 September 2008.

---

123 Eurostat, *Which sector is the main employer in the EU Member States*, 24 October 2017.

4. A gradual reform plan

In a European Commission Reflection Paper,[124] likely scenarios of the evolution of public finance in the European Union are examined in depth; among these, one named *Doing much more together* appears as the most significant. This takes into account the challenges that the Union has to face – not only the resources that should be made available to finance a Stabilization Fund and to promote the convergence and a higher competitiveness of the European economy, but also the management of problems of internal and external security, of humanitarian aid and of sustainable growth. Within this scenario an increased size of the budget is foreseen alongside a higher ceiling for own resources, backed by the definition of new sources of revenue that should be finalised to pursue the Union's policy goals.

This point had been already underlined with great emphasis in the Monti Report on the financing of the European budget[125] that correctly pointed out that new taxes can only be introduced if they are targeted at supporting the production of European public goods. This principle is correct since, in this current phase of history, the global size of public finances in Member States seems to have reached a point where it is unthinkable to further increase fiscal burdens on citizens. New taxes must therefore be justified on the basis of the subsidiarity principle, since they are based on the production of public goods that could only be supplied efficiently at the European level, while the transfer of competences from the national level to the European, for instance in the sectors of defence and security, should bring about significant savings, so that the total fiscal burden would remain unchanged or, possibly, diminish.

The same line of reasoning has been adopted by the European Parliament that, in a Report on own resources[126] underlined that the post-2020 Multiannual Financial Framework "…will need to ensure the proper financing of EU policies and programmes with a clear value added, but also provide additional means for addressing new challenges that have already been identified in fields such as growth and jobs, competitiveness, cohesion, innovation, migration, security and defence…".

---

124 European Commission, *Reflection Paper on the Future of EU Finances*, Brussels, 28 June 2017.

125 *Future Financing of the EU*, Final Report and Recommendations of the High Level Group on Own Resources (Mario Monti Chairman), Brussels, December 2016.

126 European Parliament, *Draft Report on reform of the European Union's system of own resources*, 2017 /2053(INI), Rapporteurs G. Deprez, J. Lewandowski, Brussels, 10 January 2018.

In Member States, fiscal receipts are largely targeted at financing the administrative machine and some policies that absorb a high amount of resources, but are managed more efficiently at the national level – such as welfare, education, justice and, up to now, security and defence policies. However, at the European level the revenue collected through the tax system should be settled on satisfying policy objectives that are strictly connected with the production of public goods that cannot be produced efficiently in Member States. European own resources should, therefore, guarantee a high European value added[127] and show more and more the characteristics of a price for the production of public goods, according to a theoretical scheme that goes back to De Viti De Marco.[128] Evidently, the definition of this price assumes some compliance with pre-requisites – horizontal and vertical equity, revenue stability, transparency, low cost of collection – so that the efficiency of European public finance is guaranteed together with the satisfaction of the demand for essential public goods.

The reform of the structure of financing the European budget should proceed naturally with careful gradualism, respecting a series of constraints. The production of new European public goods required by the pursuit of internal and external security, by the evolution of the global economy and by the current technological revolution, should be guaranteed, but at the same time the availability of resources needed for balancing Member States' budgets must be ensured, while the overall fiscal burden in Europe and in Member States must be kept unchanged – or possibly reduced.

The reform should be started with suitable caution, in quantitative terms as well, but anticipating right from the beginning that new taxes could be introduced to finance the European budget, if the need for higher European expenditures were to make it unavoidable. Member States could thus take into account what the structural regime of the European public finance would be, considering that in the future the financial needs of three level of governments – European, national and sub-national – would need to be satisfied. Public opinion, once it is guaranteed that the fiscal burden would remain unchanged, could then evaluate in terms of effi-

---

127 "European value added must be at the core of the discussion. On one hand, European value added is about achieving the objectives set out in Treaty; on the other it is about a budget that provides for public goods of a European dimension or helps uphold our basic freedoms, the Single Market or the Economic and Monetary Union". (European Commission, *Reflection Paper on the Future of EU Finances*, Brussels, 28 June 2017, p. 11).

128 "The tax is the price that every citizen pays to the State to cover the share of the cost of general public services that he will consume". (A. De Viti De Marco, *Principi di economia finanziaria*, Edizioni Scientifiche Einaudi, 1953, p. 114).

ciency and equity the overall fiscal structure that would emerge from the reform of the financing structure for the European budget.

At present, the main legislative act setting out the provisions for the own resources system, the Own Resources Decision (ORD), must be adopted by the Council acting unanimously after consulting the Parliament, and that decision would then be subject to ratification by all Member States; as such, this is one of the most substantial legislative procedures foreseen in the Treaty, making any attempt to introduce new resources for the budget very difficult.[129] However, it must be recalled that the Treaty of Lisbon introduced a new provision in respect of the adoption of the MFF: normally, "...the Council, acting in accordance with a special legislative procedure, shall adopt a regulation laying down the Multiannual Financial Framework. The Council shall act unanimously after obtaining the consent of the European Parliament, which shall be given by a majority of the component members..." (Article 312(2) TFUE). But the second subparagraph added that "...the European Council may, unanimously, adopt a decision authorising the Council to act by a qualified majority when adopting the regulation of the Council referred to in the first subparagraph...". This is the well-known *passerelle clause* that could improve the efficiency of procedures for the adoption of financial decisions,[130] taking into account also that "...the Treaty of Lisbon introduced new provisions regarding the implementing legislation on own resources, providing for the possibility of the Council adopting a regulation by qualified majority after obtaining the consent of the Parliament...".[131]

---

129 Article 311 TFEU states: "The Council, acting in accordance with a special legislative procedure, shall unanimously and after consulting the European Parliament adopt a decision laying down the provision relating to the system of own resources of the Union. In this context it may establish new categories of own resources or abolish an existing category. That decision shall not enter into force until it is approved by Member States in accordance with their respective constitutional requirements".

130 In his State of the Union Address 2017 (Brussels, 13 September 2017) President Juncker clearly affirmed: "I want decisions in the Council to be taken more often and more easily by qualified majority, with the equal involvement of the European Parliament. We do not need to change the Treaties for this. There are the so-called *passerelle clauses* in the current Treaties which allow us to move from unanimity to qualified majority voting in certain cases, provided the European Council decided unanimously to do so. I am also strongly in favour of moving to qualified majority voting for decisions on the common consolidated corporate tax base, on VAT, on fair taxes for the digital industry and on the financial transaction tax".

131 European Parliament, *Draft Report on reform of the European Union's system of own resources*, 2017 /2053(INI), Rapporteurs G. Deprez, J. Lewandowski, Brussels, 10 January 2018, point 7.

5. Progressivity in financing the EU budget

Taxation on personal income remains in Europe a competence of Member States. In the large majority of European states the goal to be achieved with this kind of taxation is to ensure progressivity in the distribution of the fiscal burden. However, this tax has gradually become a levy on labour and pension incomes, thus failing to reach its objective of guaranteeing greater participation of wealthy people in the financing of public expenditure. The suggestion of fiscal theory, that an income tax should be backed by a property tax levied on different assets, has resurfaced on the political agenda, so that rich people could be taxed to a significant degree. This idea has recently re-emerged in the public debate following the analyses of Thomas Piketty,[132] regarding the increase of inequality in income distribution.

As far as personal income taxation is concerned, one idea that could be examined is that national contributions to the European budget, whose main objective is to guarantee that a proportionality exists between the level of each Member States' GDP and the amount of resources it has to pay to the EU budget, could gradually be substituted with a surtax on national income taxes[133] – keeping the tax structure of each country unchanged – to be paid directly to the Union's budget. The opacity of the current system of financing the budget could thus be remedied, with a more transparent tax favouring a higher consciousness of the citizens about the costs of Union's policies.

Furthermore, the proportional rate of the surtax could be gradually modified by applying a progressivity coefficient, determined according to the ratio between the per capita GDP of each Member State and the average per capita GDP within the Union, so that richest Member States contribute to the financing of the Union to a larger degree than the poorest ones. In this way the proposed reform could represent a first step towards a system of *Finanzausgleich* (fiscal equalisation), that in any case, sooner or later, will emerge in parallel with the evolution of the Union towards a federal structure.

Up to now, personal income taxation has not been considered a resource that can be used for financing the European budget. In the Draft General Budget of the European Union for 2017 appropriations to be

132 T. Piketty, *Capital in the Twenty-First Century*, Harvard Univ. Press, 2014.

133 A. Majocchi, *Progressivity in Financing EU Budget*, Centro Studi sul Federalismo, Torino, Policy Paper No. 22, January 2017.

covered during the financial year amounted to c. €135 billion and the revenue deriving from GNI-based own resource (a contribution proportional to the national income of each Member State) represented 69.4% of this amount. It appears now that an agreement reforming the system of financing, providing resources through direct taxation of economic agents rather than indirectly through GNI contributions, could largely increase the transparency and the accountability of the budget.

The main reasons that justify the use of national contributions are fairness between Member States – since take-up rates are set to collect equal proportions of national income from each country – and the simplicity of the system, which guarantees budgetary balance and long-term stability. But there are many limitations to the so-called *fourth resource*, which cannot be defined perfectly as an own resource in line with the prescription of Article 311 of the Treaty on the Functioning of the European Union, which stipulates that "...the EU budget shall be financed wholly from own resources...". Furthermore, a system of bottom-up vertical grants powerfully supports the idea of *juste retour*, since it emphasises the amount that is being transferred by each country to the Union and induces them to regard it as an expenditure in national budgets, that must be given back through countervailing EU expenditures flowing to each Member State.

In a recent contribution to the High Level Group on Own Resources,[134] the authors considered the possibility of building some degree of cross-country redistribution using the financing instruments. More specifically, they said that "...if there is to be a reform of at least some of the expenditure items, or else if the tax instrument selected as a new own resource has some undesirable regressive properties, it may be that an appropriate automatic correction mechanism could be found in a simple, progressive schedule applied to the remaining GNI resource...". They illustrated this suggestion with a hypothetical example where the regressive effects of a carbon levy are at least partly offset through complementing the carbon levy with a progressive GNI national contribution.

Regarding the Union's budget, the introduction of a European surtax on national personal income taxes could be considered, as a replacement of the *fourth resource*. It is usual in many countries that the attribution to the national budget of the revenue coming from income taxation is backed by a surtax directed to financing the lower tiers of government.

[134] *Future Financing of the EU*, Final Report and Recommendations of the High Level Group on Own Resources (Mario Monti Chairman), Brussels, December 2016.

Thus, it could be foreseen that the revenue flowing to the EU budget from the *fourth resource* could be replaced by another surtax, that could be collected in every country at rates increasing with the rise of GDP in the country, leaving the scale of rates applied at the national level untouched, to align with domestic preferences on optimal income distribution. A system of financing the Union's budget could thus be implemented that guarantees greater transparency and, at the same time, a limited progressivity in the distribution of the fiscal burden targeted to financing European expenditures, with a higher burden for rich countries where – with equal rates and thanks to the higher level of taxable income – a greater quantity of public goods could be provided to citizens.

According to this proposal, the total revenue (T_E) to be raised through this surtax – defined, much like the *fourth resource*, as the difference between the level of the EU expenditures and the revenue of the other traditional own resources, including VAT-based own resource – is initially distributed among the Member States according to the relative share (q_i) of each country's GDP of EU GDP, as in the current system of the *fourth resource*, so that $T_i = q_i T_E$.

The amount of resources from each Member State that must be channelled to the European budget is then modified by applying a progressivity coefficient (k_i) estimated according to the ratio between the per capita income of that country and average European per capita income. The total amount of money that a country must pay to the EU budget (T_i) is finally allocated among its citizens by imposing a surtax – whose revenue will be paid directly into the EU treasury – on top of domestic income tax, without any change in national income tax systems.

To describe the nature of the proposed mechanism for financing the EU budget in a progressive way, an exercise can be developed with regard to the Draft Budget 2017, where total expenditures amount to €134.9 billion and will be covered by customs duties and sugar levies up to €20.1 billion, by VAT-based own resources up to €19.4 billion, while the residual part should be covered by the GNI-based own resources for an amount of €93.7 billion (the difference is covered by other miscellaneous revenues).

The main idea underlying this exercise is that the GNI contribution could be replaced by a progressive surtax levied on the top of national income taxes and paid directly to the EU budget. In the 2017 Draft Budget the GNI contribution was fixed at a rate t_a = 0.6232% and the amount of the GNI resource paid by each country i (T_i) is obtained by multiplying this rate by the national GNI and is equal, as a share of the total yield, to the proportion q_i of each country's national income on total European income (see Table 1, cols. 1 and 2).

The parameter chosen for a progressive distribution of this kind of taxation among EU countries is per capita income. Table 1 col. 3 shows the ratio k_i between each country's per capita income and the European average. The amount of income tax attributed to each country on a progressive basis is determined by multiplying first the proportional yield of col. 1 by the ratio k_i of col. 3. Thus, the new share $q_i{}^*$ of each country in the total yield is established (col. 4). By multiplying such a share by the total yield to be provided, the amount of income tax T_i^* for each Member State is determined (col. 5).

The weighting of the surtax on national income tax is thus different in each country. While the rate of national contributions to the EU budget was fixed at the level $t_a = 0.6232\%$, a new scale of rates now follows, ranging from 0.1246% for Bulgaria to 1.688% for Luxembourg (col. 6). The effective rate for each country equals the proportional rate multiplied by a progressivity coefficient η (col. 7), represented by the ratio between the effective share of each country in the total yield (col. 4) and the share of each country in the EU GNI (col. 2). In this way, if the effective size of the budget comes out to be greater or lower than that foreseen, the rate for each country can be simply established by multiplying the new proportional rate, fixed with regard to the level of expenditures to be covered through income taxation, by the progressivity coefficient η of col. 7. The degree of progressivity, as measured by the elasticity of the yield with regard to change in income, is high and near 2%.[135]

Having defined the distribution among Member States of the burden of income taxation, the second step is the distribution of this levy within each country among its citizens, that is reserved, in the proposed scheme, for each Member State to determine in accordance with its income tax progressivity scale, reflecting its social preference function. The distributive formula among citizens is thus considered beyond the boundaries of EU competence since, from a European standpoint, what is important is

---

135 The implicit tax function, estimated by normal cross-section regression, has the following exponential form.

$\lg T/N = -15.028 + 1.953 \lg Y/N$

$(0.564)\ (0.562)\ R^2 = 0.98$

where the figures in brackets are the standard errors of coefficient.

only the levelling of economic conditions of Member States or, at least, the reduction of regressive factors implicit in other instruments financing the EU budget.

Following the description of the proposed mechanism to reform the *fourth resource* and to incorporate a degree of progressiveness in the financing system of the European budget, the first question to be addressed is that, at first sight, it seems difficult to accept that *per capita* burden of income taxation would then differ across Member States according to the level of average income in each country, since it seems to violate the fundamental principle of *equal treatment for equals*. In this connection, it is useful to recall that the national quota of income taxation is distributed among the citizens according to the progressive scale ruling domestic taxation. Hence, it is very unlikely that the poor in a rich country pay more than the rich in a poor country. In any case, the difference in the burden of income taxation can be justified if one factors in that poor citizens of a rich Member State can exploit more opportunities and enjoy benefits which are unavailable to the citizens of a poor State, since a rich Member State can provide more services through public expenditures given the higher receipts collected, even if its rates of income taxes are similar to those of poor countries.

But there is an efficiency effect of this reform to be considered as well, since a progressive structure of taxation brings in a significant incentive to reduce disequilibria inside the Union. In particular, rich countries have an interest in the growth of per capita income in weak regions in as much as, if convergence ensues, their own burden of income taxation is reduced. Eventually, if perfect equalisation is realised, the progressivity coefficient η is 1 for all countries and the distribution of income taxation among the Member States becomes proportional. Meanwhile, weak countries have no incentive to cut down their efforts to reduce disparities in the level of income since, with a progressive income taxation, the elasticity of disposable income is less than 1, but considerably larger than zero.

It is clear that these redistributive and incentive effects will probably be weak now, given the limited size of the EU budget. But the proposed reform could probably be permitted – perhaps by initially implementing a weaker degree of progressivity – when the heavy tasks put on the shoulders of the Union, in order to face the new challenges of migration, security and foreign aid, and the support to economic growth after the long period of stagnation following the crisis started in 2008, will demand a larger budget for the Union.

6. The theory behind the progressive surtax

The model of fiscal federalism normally referred to in the literature is that initially developed by Musgrave,[136] further elaborated by Oates.[137] In this model the redistribution function must be centralised because personal mobility, which is inversely proportional to the size of a given territory,[138] may cause locally managed redistribution policy to fail. In fact, poor taxpayers would have a strong incentive to move to areas where redistribution measures are substantial, with subsidies for less favoured income earners and high rates of taxation on the highest income, whilst the rich will concentrate in areas where redistribution policy is weaker. As a consequence, financial resources will be depleted in areas with an effective redistribution policy, since expenditure is very high while the tax base shrinks, whereas in the richest areas the budget will be in huge surplus because the tax base will increase.

This theoretical scheme is contradicted by the present assignment of economic functions within the European Union, because redistribution policy is, and probably will remain in the foreseeable future, a competence of the Member States, and not of the Union. In the literature, following the well-known paper on redistribution as a local public good by Pauly,[139] theoretical reasons have been put forward in support of this choice; in Europe the assignment seems reasonable owing to the wide differences still persisting at the national level among preference functions concerning the optimal level of redistribution. This reasoning was further developed by Tresch,[140] who assigned the task of income redistribution among different regional areas to the central tier, while the lower levels of government keep responsibility for interpersonal redistribution.[141]

The Tresch model assumes that the welfare level of local and regional governments is affected only by the benefits to those individuals resident within their jurisdiction, excluding any linkage among welfare functions of different areas. It also assumes that individuals' benefits depend only

136 R.A. Musgrave, *The Theory of Public Finance*, McGraw-Hill, New York, 1959.

137 W. Oates, *Fiscal Federalism*, Harcourt Brace Jovanovich, New York, 1972.

138 The larger the territory, the lower the rate of mobility – and inversely.

139 M.V. Pauly, "Income redistribution as a Local Public Good", in *Journal of Public Economics*, 1973, Vol. 2, No. 1, pp. 35-58.

140 R.W. Tresch, *Public Finance. A Normative Approach*, Business Publications Inc., Plano, 1981.

141 A. Majocchi, "Le fédéralisme fiscal et la fonction redistributive: le cas de la Communauté européenne", in *Revue française de finances publiques*, 1987, No. 20, pp. 137-155.

on the goods they consume, excluding any externalities. In contrast, the welfare of the central government is related only to the welfare of the lower tiers of government, measured according to their own welfare functions and dependent on the benefits of their citizens. The assignment of the redistribution competence is radically modified with respect to the traditional model by the constraint – with which the central government is obliged to comply – of non-interference with the welfare functions of local governments and by the assumption of the lack of interdependence and externalities: only local governments redistribute income among individuals according to their own preferences, while central government uses lump-sum transfers to equalise the incomes of different regions according to its own welfare functions.

Table 1

	T_i	q_i	k_i	q_i^*	T_i^*	t_a^*	η
	[1]	[2]	[3]	[4]	[5]	[6]	[7]
Belgium	2649.8	2.83	1.271	3.12	2923	0.6871	1.102
Bulgaria	278.7	0.3	0.2187	0.06	56.2	0.1246	0.2
Czech Republic	987.8	1.05	0.5486	0.50	468.4	0.2968	0.476
Denmark	1765.4	1.88	1.6597	2.71	2538.9	0.8983	1.441
Germany	20024.9	21.37	1.2881	23.88	22372.3	0.6963	1.117
Estonia	134.6	0.14	0.5347	0.07	65.6	0.3116	0.5
Ireland	1143.5	1.22	1.9131	2.03	1901.8	1.037	1.664
Greece	1122.3	1.2	0.5625	0.58	543.4	0.3012	0.483
Spain	7104.9	7.58	0.8055	5.3	4965.4	0.4357	0.699
France	14207.7	15.16	1.1388	14.98	14034.2	0.6158	0.988
Croatia	284.3	0.3	0.3611	0.09	84.3	0.1870	0.3
Italy	10489.8	11.2	0.9375	9.10	8525.5	0.5063	0.812
Cyprus	110.8	0.12	0.7222	0.07	65.6	0.3635	0.583
Latvia	166.4	0.18	0.4270	0.06	56.2	0.2077	0.333
Lithuania	248.1	0.26	0.4479	0.10	93.7	0.2397	0.416
Luxembourg	225.6	0.24	3.121	0.65	609	1.688	2.708
Hungary	706.5	0.75	0.3854	0.25	234.2	0.2077	0.333
Malta	59.0	0.06	0.7049	0.04	37.5	0.4155	0.666
Netherlands	4422.7	4.72	1.388	5.68	5321.4	0.7499	1.203
Austria	2119.8	2.26	1.368	2.68	2510.8	0.7390	1.186
	T_i	q_i	k_i	q_i^*	T_i^*	t_a^*	η
	[1]	[2]	[3]	[4]	[5]	[6]	[7]
Poland	2666.1	2.84	0.3888	0.96	899.4	0.2106	0.338
Portugal	1145.1	1.22	0.6006	0.64	599.6	0.3269	0.524
Romania	1084.4	1.16	0.2812	0.28	262.3	0.1504	0.241
Slovakia	246.8	0.26	0.5034	0.11	103.1	0.2637	0.423
Slovenia	497.3	0.53	0.6493	0.3	281.1	0.3527	0.566
Finland	1289.6	1.38	1.326	1.58	1480.2	0.7135	1.145
Sweden	3057.0	3.26	1.5833	4.47	4187.8	0.8545	1.371
United Kingdom	15446.4	16.49	1.375	19.66	18418.8	0.743	1.192
European Union	93685.3	100.00		100.00	93639.7		
	(million €)				(million €)		

This model seems to provide adequate theoretical support for proposals to finance the Union's budget with a surtax on top of national personal income taxes levied by each Member State. The Union's surtax, levied according to the level of GDP of each Member State, but with a rate corrected with a progressive index, fulfils the task of income redistribution assigned to the central government and does not interfere with the progressiveness scale characterising each national income tax system, that is related to the redistribution task assigned in the Tresch model to the local authorities according to their own preferences.

From the point of view of the effectiveness of fiscal policy, the advantages of this scheme can be summed up in three points:

a) transparency of the tax: citizens know the fiscal burden linked to the funding of the Union's budget. This point becomes important if the size of the European budget were expected to increase gradually in the future;
b) redistribution effects: this kind of taxation has a positive redistribution impact on the various areas within the Union that do not have homogenous levels of economic development, and it may represent a first step towards a European *Finanzausgleich* system, with large equalising impact;
c) stabilisation effects: a tax related to income levels strengthens the automatic stabilisation properties of the budget. The measure of stabilisation effects depends significantly on the amount of total revenue and the technical characteristics of the tax, if the latter is structured so that the time lag between income and tax changes is minimised. A further advantage of this proposal is that it does not require prior harmonisation of existing national laws on income taxation.

7. New sources of revenue for the EU budget

The European Commission has presented the first proposal for the next Multiannual Financial Framework 2021-2027,[142] whose goal is to specify the spending limits for each category of expenditure and to guarantee that the long-term budget provides adequate funds for the Union's priorities. The global amount suggested in this proposal amounts to €1,279 billion in com-

142 European Commission, *A Modern Budget for a Union that Protects, Empowers and Defends*, COM(2018) 321final, Brussels, 2 May 2018.

mitments expressed at market prices over the whole period, equivalent to 1.11% of the EU GNI. This level of commitments translates into payment appropriations reaching €1,246 billion, or 1.08% of GNI. In real terms, the future long-term budget is broadly similar to the current one, taking into account the inclusion of the European Development Fund, and foresees a redeployment of expenditures in favour of new and pressing priorities, but without increasing in a significant measure the size of expenditures.

According to the Commission's proposal the budget should be funded by traditional own resources (custom duties, a simplified current Value Added Tax applying a uniform call rate on a standard rated base and GNI contributions), but also by a basket of new own resources: 20% of the revenues from Emission Trading System (excluding ETS allowances for aviation), with an estimated annual average revenues that could vary between €1.2 and €3.0 billion depending on the market price for ETS allowances; a 3% call rate applied to the new Common Consolidated Corporate Tax Base, that could bring an annual average of approximately €12 billion; and a national contribution calculated on the amount of non-recycled plastic packaging waste in each Member State that, by applying a call rate of €0.80 per kilo, could bring around €7 billion. These resources will provide annually receipts equal to around €22 billion, or 12% of total revenues. But over the last few years many other suggestions have been advanced for shaping a new financing system of the EU budget.

7.1. Financial Transactions Tax

In recent years the size of the financial sector has hugely increased, compared with the real economy. This development has been favoured by the liberalisation of capital movements and, most of all, by the deregulation of financial markets promoted firstly by Ronald Reagan in the United States and by Margaret Thatcher in the UK. In 2011 the European Commission put forward the proposal of a Directive concerning the structure of a common tax on financial transactions. From a political point of view, this was justified given widespread public opinion that the financial system was largely responsible for the economic crisis. From a legal point of view, the justification rested on the basis of Article 113 of the TFEU, since the rules proposed were directed towards harmonising legislation with regard to the taxation of financial transactions, so that the proper functioning of the internal market would be assured and distortions of competition – due to delocalisation of economic activities brought about by the diversity of fiscal systems – avoided.

The Commission's proposal was later withdrawn, lacking sufficient support in the Council. As a matter of fact, given the fierce competition at the global level for a larger share of available financial resources, the implementation in Europe of some kind of taxation levied on the financial sector, even if reasonable in the medium term,[143] appears to be naturally condemned to be pushed back to a later phase of the reform process. In any case, this kind of taxation should be defined at the European level with common rules to prevent avoidance and fiscal competition, keeping in mind that the priority objective is financial stability, that could only be guaranteed with a common European initiative.

In the Monti Report it is assumed that for the banking sector the common tax base proposed by the Commission for the Corporation Income Tax could also be used,[144] or a *Financial Activity Tax* could be introduced,[145] "...which would target the base of the *value added* of financial services which has been so far exempted from the VAT...". But, having underlined that the tax would provide advantages in terms of efficiency in the functioning of the Banking Union ensuring "...a level playing field in the area of taxation...", the political costs of this choice were stressed, since the possibility of reaching a consensus between the Member States was limited in the short term. Nonetheless, "...in the medium-term perspective of a reform of the whole system of own resources, it may make sense to move from the financing with risk specific fees to a financing based on corporate income tax or on value added...".

In his speech at the Sorbonne, President Emmanuel Macron, having expressed his hope that a partnership with Africa would become an essential part in the recovery of the European project, proposed a new structure for a European tax on financial transactions to collect the resources needed to fund a growth plan for Africa. Macron observed that Great Britain had already implemented a similar measure – Stamp Duty; then, "...if we decide together to adopt the British tax, nobody could say that competitive disadvantages could follow for the European Union...". A similar tax, with a moderate rate, but with a large tax base, could represent a first

143 "The financial transaction tax could be designed to reinforce the single market, mirror the benefits of the internal market for the largest companies and strengthen the fight against the tax fraud and tax evasion" (European Commission, *Reflection Paper on the Future of EU Finances*, Brussels, 28 June 2017, p. 29). In this document the same evaluation is referred to the "common corporate tax base".

144 European Commission, *Building a fair, competitive and stable corporate tax system for the EU*, COM(2016) 682 final, Strasbourg, 25 October 2016.

145 *Future Financing of the EU*, *op. cit.*, p. 52.

step towards the introduction of a tax on financial transactions, that could provide considerable resources for the European budget.

7.2. Value Added Tax

Revenues from Value Added Tax as an own resource for the EU budget are currently around €15-20 billion per year, a level which could be maintained with the simplified procedure suggested by the Commission[146] by adjusting the call rate upwards – presently 0.3% on a base capped at 50% of GNI – accordingly. In the Monti report two alternatives were considered – the first foresees the application of an equal fixed rate in all Member States, while the second involves the enlargement of a harmonised taxable base as well – which will represent a significant development of this kind of levy, with a positive relevant impact on the fight against fraud.[147] That a part of VAT revenues is paid directly to the Union's budget seems justified, not only since the VAT structure is already common to all Member States, being determined by a European Directive, but also since Economic and Monetary Union should have at its disposal a fiscal instrument to control the trend of consumption expenditures, firstly for anti-cyclical purposes and, secondly, for environmental objectives.

The European growth model should not be linked to a continuous increase in private goods consumption. Ecological equilibrium requires that, if a higher quantity of resources should be made available to developing countries in order to guarantee a progressive approach of their living standards towards the level of the richest countries, then in the industrialised world the share of savings that will finance the increased investments needed to support productivity and to improve the quality of life should be greater. The goal of sustainable development is already a basic value for the European Union.[148]

---

146 European Commission, *Proposal for a Council Decision on the System of Own resources of the European Union*, COM(2018) 325 final, Brussels, 2 May 2018.

147 "Annual estimates of VAT fraud are indeed higher than the annual EU budget. In 2013 the VAT gap – the difference between the expected VAT revenue and VAT actually collected in Member States – was almost €170 billion" (*Future Financing of the EU*, Final Report and Recommendations of the High Level Group on Own Resources (Mario Monti Chairman), Brussels, December 2016, p. 55).

148 Article 3 paragraph 3 of the Treaty on European Union states: "The Union [...] shall work for the sustainable development of Europe based on balanced economic growth and price stability, a highly competitive social market economy, aiming at full employment and social progress, and a high level of protection and improvement of the quality of the environment".

Macroeconomic equilibrium rules demand that in rich countries savings exceed investments and the surplus in the trade balance should be employed to finance aid to less developed countries where, if growth is to be promoted, investments must necessarily be higher than savings. For Europe, this implies the financing of a Marshall Plan for Africa, whose objective should be not only to favour the development of the Continent, but also to support demand for European goods. Consequently, the attribution of a part of VAT revenue to the European budget is justified by the need, from one side, to have at its disposal an instrument to guarantee economic stability and ecological equilibrium and, from the other side, to provide the financial resources necessary to promote growth of less developed countries at the world level.

7.3. Corporation Income Tax

The starting point for a reform of corporation income tax is identified as a harmonisation of the tax base, and by the definition of a minimum level of taxation, to avoid the phenomenon of fiscal competition that might negatively affect the markets' efficiency. Subsequently, it would be possible to envisage the attribution of a part of the receipts to the Union's budget, targeted at developing a European industrial policy.

In October 2016 the Commission proposed a re-launch of the Common Consolidated Corporate Tax Base (CCCTB),[149] through a two-stage process. In the first step, the common base would be implemented, with consolidation put in place swiftly afterwards. The CCCTB would be mandatory for large groups, with consolidated group revenues of more than €750 million. Cross-border companies would benefit from a single set of rules to calculate their profits in the EU, rather than a combination of different national systems. They would be able to file a single tax return for all their EU activities through a *One-Stop-Shop* system, dealing with just one Member State rather than multiple tax authorities. Consolidation would also mean that losses in one Member State could be automatically set off against profits in another, thereby allowing cross-border companies to enjoy the same treatment as purely domestic ones.

An own resource based on corporate tax would be justified insofar as multinational enterprises benefit from the freedoms of the Single Market and the CCCTB would help Union efforts to tackle tax avoidance. Once

---

149 European Commission, *Building a fair, competitive and stable corporate tax system for the EU*, COM(2016) 682 final, Strasbourg, 25 October 2016.

the CCCTB has been agreed in line with the Commission's proposals of 2016, a new own resource based on it with a call rate of 3% for the EU could bring an annual average income of approximately €12 billion.

7.4. Digital Tax

The need to plan for the introduction of a Digital Tax has recently emerged in the political debate. According to the principles of taxation at the international level, the essential requirement for taxing non-resident firms is the principle of permanent establishment. But with the explosion of the digital economy and the parallel processes of dematerialisation of economic activity, production can take place anywhere, far from the consumption markets, and taxation can be avoided with the absence of a permanent organisation. To deter avoidance and distortions with regard to markets' efficiency it seems reasonable to evaluate the introduction at the European level of a withholding tax on the turnover of digital transactions or a specific tax on the consumption of digital goods. In any case, cooperative solutions and a coordination at the continental level certainly seem to be preferred, to guarantee efficiency and equity.

The European economy faces a boom in digital business, but current tax rules are not designed to cater for those companies that are global, virtual or have little or no physical presence. Nine of the world's top 20 companies by market capitalisation are digital; the challenge is to ensure that digital companies contribute their fair share of tax, as it stands digital companies have an average effective tax rate half that of the traditional economy in the EU. Two distinct legislative initiatives have been proposed by the Commission,[150] aiming towards a fairer taxation of digital activities. The first initiative aims to reform corporate tax rules so that Member States could tax profits that are generated in their territory, even if a company does not have a physical presence there.[151] This forms the Commission's long-term preferred solution.

---

150 European Commission, *Proposal for a Council Directive laying down rules relating to the corporate taxation of a significant digital presence*, COM(2018) 147 final, Brussels 21 March 2018; European Commission, *Proposal for a Council Directive on the common system of a digital services tax on revenues resulting from the provision of certain digital services*, COM(2018) 148 final, Brussels, 21 March 2018.

151 A digital platform will be deemed to have a taxable 'digital presence' or a virtual permanent establishment in a Member State if it fulfils one of these three criteria: a) it exceeds a threshold of €7million in annual revenues in a Member State; b) it has more than 100,000 users in a Member State in a taxable year; c) over 3000 business contracts for digital services are created between the company and business users in a taxable year.

The second proposal is in response to calls from a number of Member States[152] for an interim tax, which covers the main digital activities that currently escape tax altogether in the EU.[153] This indirect tax would apply to the turnover generated by certain digital activities which escape the current tax framework entirely. Tax revenues would be collected by Member States where the users are located and will only apply to companies with total annual worldwide revenues of €750 million. An estimated €5billion in revenues a year could be generated for Member States if the tax is applied at a rate of 3%.

152 The Economy Ministers of Germany, France, Italy and Spain at the informal Ecofin meeting in Tallinn of 15-16 September 2017 have presented the proposal to introduce an Equalisation Tax established according to the turnover generated in Europe by digital firms. If the rate were fixed in an interval between 2% and 5%, this tax could raise a revenue similar to what these firm should pay under an income tax regime. In Tallinn six other countries (Austria, Bulgaria, Greece, Portugal, Romania and Slovenia) have subscribed a political declaration for a joint initiative on taxation of firms working in the digital economy", where they underline the need to proceed rapidly and ask the Commission to put on the table a legislative proposal on the Equalisation Tax.

153 "We estimate that close to 40% of multinational profits are shifted to low-tax countries each year. Profits shifting is highest among US multinationals; the tax revenue losses are highest for the European Union and developing countries" (T.R. Tørsløv, L.S. Wier, G. Zucman, *The Missing Profits of Nations*, NBER Working Paper, No. 24701, June 2018).

Chapter 7

The Carbon Tax

1. The rationale behind energy taxation

In the past, environmental policy has largely relied on command-and-control measures.[154] These generally identify maximum emissions levels or minimum efficiency standards that apply equally to every economic agent through all economic sectors. If controls are cheap and efficient, regulatory measures have, as the main advantage, the possibility to ensure that environmental targets are indeed met. Especially in cases where the achievement of the target is of crucial importance (for instance, for sanitary reasons), they may be preferable to alternative instruments.

There are, however, many drawbacks associated with these regulatory instruments:

- from the point of view of static efficiency, if a standard for emission reduction is set, every firm will have to make equal reduction efforts, regardless of the fact that marginal reduction costs could differ among polluters. It would be cheaper for the economy as a whole if firms with relatively low marginal reduction costs were forced to reduce emissions more than firms with high costs, because total costs in this case would be minimised;
- from the point of view of dynamic efficiency, with direct regulations a firm is not penalised for emitting a residual amount of pollution as long as the firm complies with the standard. Therefore, firms have no incentive to use new technologies to reduce emissions below the norm set by the regulatory authority. Conversely, under a tax regime polluting firms have to pay taxes on the remaining amount of pollution. This will stimulate them to look for and adopt

[154] For a comparison between taxes and command-and-control measures: A.L. Bovenberg, L.H. Goulder, *Environmental Taxation and Regulation*, NBER Working Paper 8458, Cambridge MA, September 2001.

new reduction technologies, thereby reducing their tax burden, since firms have a cost incentive to reduce polluting emissions as much as possible, otherwise they face high tax payments.

If these are the basic reasons for adopting tax measures for environmental purposes, it is important to identify on what specific grounds it is possible to support the adoption of an energy tax. It is well known that in this field an instrument that traditionally has been implemented in many different countries is the excise on mineral oils, whose main purpose has been to raise revenue, given the low demand elasticity for this kind of commodity. It is only recently that excise on mineral oils has been also considered as an instrument of environmental policy, especially with regard to transport.

The debate on the use of an energy tax has been reinvigorated with the growing awareness of the problems of global warming. If the aim of the envisaged policy is exclusively to cut down emissions of carbon dioxide, the prime instrument, from an economic point of view, is a pure carbon tax as opposed to an energy tax. Here, the reduction of CO_2 emissions is achieved in three ways:

- a reduction of energy usage in households and firms, induced by the higher relative prices of energy;
- rising energy prices provide an incentive to improve the efficiency of energy usage both in end-use sectors and in the production sector of secondary energies;
- fuel substitution leads to replacement of carbon-intensive fuels by low or no-carbon intensive alternatives, especially in electricity production where significant possibilities exist. However, this option is also available in end-use sectors (*e.g.* the substitution of coal for heating by natural gas or fuel oil).

A pure carbon tax links the tax burden on various energy products to their carbon content perfectly, through all three options described above. An energy tax leads to little fuel substitution. Hence, compared to an energy tax, a carbon tax needs a lower tax rate to reach the same target of reduction of carbon dioxide emissions because carbon-intensive fuels are made relatively more expensive.

But an energy tax would also reduce many other environmental impacts. In a world without externalities it would make no sense to tax energy as such, as this would only distort the optimal allocation of resources. However, an energy tax might be strongly advocated as energy consumption is, in fact, related to a number of important externalities such as acid rain, transport related externalities (*e.g.* congestion) and externalities related with the use of nuclear energy. Even if energy tax is not a premier instrument, since the link between externality and energy use is not perfect, it seems to be in any case an attractive second-best solution.

Furthermore, an energy tax in an integrated internal market, such as the European Union, would reduce the differences in the impact of taxation among Member States that a carbon tax would bring about, since CO_2 concentrations differ more importantly across countries than energy use. In conclusion, even if a pure carbon tax has a major impact on the reduction of CO_2 emissions, energy taxation could be supported by considerations related to the overall impact on total welfare, which is largely influenced by side effects on other variables too (*e.g.* other environmental externalities, income distribution, etc.). Hence, it is hardly unexpected that countries implementing energy taxation for environmental purposes have adopted in some cases a combination of a pure energy and carbon taxes, trying to achieve a number of environmental targets with the same instrument.

2. A first European proposal of an energy-carbon tax

The problem of global warming currently represents one of the principal areas of concern for all mankind. CO_2 emissions are considered to be the main contributory factor to the greenhouse effect (its share of total greenhouse gases amounts to 65% according to recent estimates);[155] this atmospheric concentration of carbon dioxide is largely of anthropogenic origin, primarily caused by the burning of fossil fuels. Also, the depletion of tropical rain forests has become a major source of atmospheric concentration of carbon dioxide in the last years, and it is now estimated, together with agriculture and other land use, to be responsible for 24% of emissions.

While global warming is a world-wide problem, the main responsibility lies with industrialised countries. In 2016, world emissions of carbon dioxide reach 36,183 million tonnes (mt).[156] In the United States CO_2 emissions are evaluated at 5,312mt, while in the EU28 are equivalent to 3,499mt and in Japan to 1,209mt; but it is important to remark that

155 www.epa.gov/ghgemissions/global-greenhouse-gas-emissions-data.

156 The reported data can be found on: www.globalcarbonatlas.org/en/CO2-emissions.

emissions in China (10,151mt), are almost double that in the United States, in Russia they are 1,635mt and in India these reach 2,431mt. In the near future policy measures needed for curbing carbon dioxide emissions should especially be implemented in Northern industrialised countries. But, with the expected economic growth of developing countries, their CO_2 emissions could increase dramatically, since energy efficiency is significantly at very low level. An effective policy for addressing the global warming problem should therefore provide the right economic incentives to industrialised countries for increasing energy efficiency and limiting carbon dioxide emissions, but at the same time it should warrant adequate incentives for raising energy efficiency in less developed countries as well.

The European Union contribution to global CO_2 emissions is only 9.67%, compared to 14.7% for the US, 3.34% for Japan, 28.05% for China, 4.52% for Russia and 6.72% for India. Any unilateral action by the EU would not solve the greenhouse problem, whose nature is global. But with the adoption of the Convention on Climate Change at the UNCED Earth Summit held in Rio in June 1992 and, afterwards, with the approval of the Kyoto Protocol and the Agreement reached within the COP21 (held in December 2015 in Paris), a world-wide commitment to cope with the problem of global warming has been taken. It is within this framework that the best instruments to achieve the goal in the most cost-effective way should be chosen.

In the case of climate change there is no clear-cut trade-off between regulation and taxation. A comprehensive strategy must give space both to command-and-control and to economic instruments, relying on a mutually reinforcing set of regulatory and fiscal measures. Energy efficiency could be promoted through higher energy prices and the imposition of technical standards, while fuel-switching towards the use of less-polluting energy sources could be favoured by an increase of energy prices according to the carbon content. In the industrial sector some residual space remains for voluntary agreements targeted at a reduction of CO_2 emissions.

Within the European Union, as a first step to limiting greenhouse gases, the joint Energy-Environment Council of 29 September 1990 decided to stabilise CO_2 emissions in the Community by the year 2000 at the 1990 level. To reach this target, the strategy initially proposed by the Commission aimed at balancing the competitive needs of the European economy with environmental requirements; the policy suggestions involved a broad range of different measures.

First of all, the possibility to improve energy efficiency appeared to exist in all sectors and for all energy sources. This *no-regret policy* would increase energy security, improve the transport system, limit energy-related air emissions other than CO_2 and strengthen the industrial structure. But fuel switching also has a major role to play, especially in the medium and long term, developing a much more substantial share of natural gas to the detriment of coal and possibly oil. Finally, the contribution to achieving the stabilisation target through an increased use of renewable energy sources should be promoted, by overcoming technical obstacles with R&D programmes and by improving the economic position of these energies.

Hence, regulatory measures were needed to exploit the possible gains in energy efficiency, while R&D programmes should be promoted to keep up minimum-emissions power production from fossil sources – including the development of carbon abatement technologies – renewable energy sources and efficient energy utilisation and conservation, including energy-efficient transport. A list of more than 40 measures was included in the European Climate Change Programme,[157] launched in June 2000.

In 1992 the Commission proposed to supplement this set of regulatory measures with a fiscal levy on the use of all non-renewable energies (including large scale hydro-electric), thus providing a signal to the market of the upward trend of energy prices, and influencing in this way the behaviours of firms and individuals. This tax was considered to be perfectly consistent with the *polluter pays principle*. Furthermore, it is a well-known conclusion of the existing literature on environmental taxation that, since CO_2 emissions are related to very different uses of fossil fuels by a very large number of consumers and business, the use of policy instruments based on market mechanism to provide incentives for the reduction of CO_2 emissions would certainly be more cost-effective than relying solely on regulatory measures.

3. The design of the energy/carbon tax

In defining a carbon-energy tax proposal[158] the Commission had to consider the following basic options:

a) a production tax or an import excise. Since the production (or importing) of fossil fuels is unequally spread over the territory of

[157] European Commission, *European Climate Change Programme, Report 2001*, Brussels, 2001.

[158] European Commission, *Proposal for a Council Directive introducing a tax on carbon dioxide emissions and energy*, COM(92) 226 final, 30 June 1992.

the Member States, a genuine production/import tax would not reflect the consumption of energy products and the amount of CO_2 emissions of each Member State. Excises are a consumption tax which could be levied on the domestic producers (or importers) of the energy products as well as on the final or intermediate energy consumers. It seems the most convenient system for taxing energy. The early application in the production process combines the advantage that the number of economic agents performing the taxable transactions is small and easily verifiable and that the burden of the tax is immediately shifted onto all energy consumers, thereby directly affecting their behaviours. If the revenue were credited to the Member States where consumption takes place, for intra-Community transactions the levy has to be postponed until the goods have reached the Member State of destination and are released for consumption, requiring a system of administrative follow-up of the goods – also for the products currently not submitted to excises – from the production (or import) site to the Member State of consumption. This problem would not emerge if the revenue were attributed to the Union's budget;

b) taxable products. For gas and liquid fuels, the tax base and the corresponding rates should be related to individual products as defined in the Combined Nomenclature.[159] For coal different categories have to be defined, each with a specific emission factor. The introduction of an average rate for coal would favour the most polluting qualities of coal and lead to serious distortions in competition, since the quality of coal is often linked with geographical factors. Taxable products should include brown coal (lignite) and peat;

c) carbon/energy share of the tax. The tax proposal would have an energy component – to be applied to all energies – and a component based on carbon content of each fossil fuel. The energy tax would be more effective in promoting energy efficiency. The carbon tax would provide more specific incentives to reduce CO_2 emissions, while putting a relatively higher burden on coal, which is the most polluting – even if the most secure – energy supply. At the same time, this would favour nuclear energy, which has advantages in terms of CO_2 reduction, even if it leads to its own particular problems (security, waste disposal). Furthermore, the impact of the

[159] The Combined Nomenclature (CN) is a tool for classifying goods, set up to meet the requirements both of the Common Customs Tariff and of the EU's external trade statistics.

carbon tax on the industrial competitive position of the Member States would be different according to their energy structure;

d) tax base. The tax base must be defined at the the stage where the various products acquire their definitive characteristics – from the point of view of CO_2 emissions and energy content. This is a technical requirement – otherwise downstream differentiation would have to be introduced – and at the same time guarantees a clear link between the tax base and the environmental/energy targets. Accordingly, the tax base should be defined in a way as to include fossil fuels used for combustion, considering that:
   - petroleum products acquire their definitive attributes when processed into various types of mineral oils;
   - natural gas and coal broadly acquire these when extracted – even if they could be further processed;

e) tax rates. If the main goal of the tax is to stabilise CO_2 emissions, the target rate must be established in real terms, combined with a minimum initial rate indexed to the consumer price level. This tax rate should be additional to existing taxes that are levied on some products – *e.g.* the excise on mineral oil;

f) exemptions. A zero rate should be established for energy sources used as raw materials and for renewable energies (with the further provision that electricity produced by large hydro-plants should be subject to the energy tax). A special fiscal treatment should be provided in favour of energy intensive industrial sectors largely open to international trade, that accept to limit CO_2 emissions through voluntary agreements;

g) *ad hoc* system for electricity. Different options are open for taxing electricity:
   - Option 1: pure input tax. Fossil fuels supplied to power stations are submitted to excise taxation, while an analogous tax is levied on nuclear heat and hydraulic force. The main advantage of this option is that it promotes energy efficiency through a complete taxation of conversion losses, which are considerable. If the revenue is attributed to national budgets, this option does not comply with the destination principle and requires a system of rebates for exempted sectors or firms.
   - Option 2: output tax. Fossil fuels supplied to power stations are exempted from the excise and electricity is taxed on its own as an energy product. There is perfect compliance with the desti-

nation principle, but there is no (positive) incentive to improve energy efficiency in power generation plants, whereas a (negative) incentive is provided for a substitution of other fuels with electricity. In addition, there is a problem in how to assess the carbon tax, since the electricity supplied is made out of different fuels.

- Option 3: a combined solution. Electricity is taxed on its own on the basis of the energy content, taking into account conversion losses, and the price charged to the consumers includes – besides the energy tax – the carbon tax paid according to the carbon content of the fossil fuels supplied to the power stations. This option – that lies behind the solution adopted in the Commission's 1992 proposal – could easily comply with the destination principle. Furthermore, while the carbon tax provides an incentive to enhance efficiency in the production of electricity and to reduce CO_2 emissions, the energy tax, being immediately charged on prices paid by consumers, affects their behaviour towards more energy-saving and allows for a zero or reduced rate to be charged to energy-intensive sectors, without having to implement a system of rebates.

The Commission's proposal favoured a balanced solution, 50% of the tax being modulated according to the energy content and the other 50% being modulated according to the carbon content of each type of fossil fuel. The Commission estimated that a rate of the tax equivalent to $10 per barrel of oil could be sufficient to achieve the stabilisation target,[160] when supported by other regulatory measures and by complementary

160 Theoretically, the optimal rate of a carbon tax should be equal to the marginal damage of CO_2 emissions brought about by the combustion of fossil fuels. But the damages are difficult to estimate correctly since climate change is a global "bad". Hence, the Commission's proposal of a rate equal in 2000, at the end of a transition period, to $ 10 per barrel of oil is a *second best* solution. First, the changes are estimated in energy consumption between 1990 and 2000 [$\Delta Q/Q$], necessary to achieve the reduction of CO_2 emissions that could guarantee emissions stabilisation in 2000 at the same level of 1990. The energy/carbon tax should be fixed at a rate that will allow, through a change in the price of energy, the attainment of this objective, given η, the demand elasticity for energy consumption [$\Delta Q/Q \,.\, (P/\Delta P)$]. Therefore, the tax rate should be exactly what is sufficient to guarantee the needed price variation ΔP, and it could be derived given the demand elasticity and the objective to be reached. It will be equal to: $\Delta P = (\Delta Q/Q).(P/\eta)$. At the time the proposal was put forward, given a current price of $ 20 per barrel of oil, $\eta = 0.2$ and $\Delta Q/Q = 0.10$, it followed that $t = \Delta P = \$10$ per barrel of oil.

national programmes. This tax rate could be progressively reached by the year 2000, starting with a rate of \$3 and increasing it by \$1 each year. This provision would be important in promoting a gradual adaptation of the European economy to the new conditions of the energy market. The proposal established that the tax rate would be Ecu 2.81 per tonne of carbon dioxide emitted by fossil fuels and Ecu 0.21 per gigajoule as regards the energy component. This would represent a total tax of Ecu 17.7 per tonne of oil equivalent (toe), corresponding to \$3 per barrel at 1991 prices.[161] However, electricity would attract energy tax at the rate of Ecu 2.1 per MWh,[162] with the exception of electricity generated by hydroelectric installations, that will be taxed at the rate of Ecu 0.76 per MWh.

The new tax would have to be decided at the European level and introduced by the Member States, with the revenue accruing to their Treasuries, while avoiding any risk of trade distortions within the internal market, since the legislation would be implemented at the national level according to a European Directive. A key characteristic of the tax would be its revenue neutrality; it should not result in any increase in total tax burden and the resulting revenue would need to be offset by fiscal incentives and by tax reductions.[163] The goal to be reached by this shift of the burden of

---

161 At the rate of exchange of 1991 (Ecu 1 = \$ 1.242), a tax rate of \$ 3 per barrel of oil is equivalent to Ecu 17.7 per toe [\$3(7.33)/1.242], since 1 toe = 7.33 barrels. Energy tax share (50% of the total) is equal to Ecu 0.21 per GJ, since half of the total tax (Ecu 8.85) should be divided by 41.468 (1 toe = 41.868 gigajoules). The carbon share of the tax (50%) will be Ecu 10.33 per tC [8.85.(1.168)], since 1 tC = 1.168 toe, and Ecu 2.81 per tCO_2 (10.33/3.66) since 1 tC = 3.66 tCO_2.

162 Since 3,600 GJ = 1 GWh and the tax rate is ECU 0.21 per GJ, the tax to be paid for each GWh equals 0.21 (3,600) = ECU 756, or ECU 0.756 per MWh, since 1 GW = 1,000 MW. This is the rate foreseen in the Commission's proposal for electricity generated by hydroelectric installations. But, since the average efficiency of electricity production, taking into account conversion losses, could be estimated equal to 36.2%, the rate will be equal to ECU 0.756(100)/36.2 = ECU 2.1 per MWh. Given this value for the efficiency of electricity produced with the use of fossil fuels, implying that with an input of 100 MW the output of electricity is 36.2 MW, this means that the outcome is the same by taxing energy input [0.756 (100 MW)] = ECU 756 per MW or output of electricity [36.2 (ECU 2.1)] = ECU 756 per MW.

163 Since Member States are responsible for collecting and administering the energy/carbon tax, they will have to decide on the arrangements for ensuring overall neutrality. These arrangements might include reduction in direct taxation, in social security contributions or in indirect taxation. In the Delors White Paper (European Commission, *Growth, Competitiveness, Employment. The Challenges and Ways Forward into the 21st Century*, White Paper, COM(93) 700, Brussels, 5 December 1993) the idea was put forward to finance with the receipts of the carbon-energy tax a reduction of the rates of social security contributions on unskilled workers, so that a double dividend (less pollution and higher employment) could be achieved.

taxation away from distortionary taxes on companies and individuals and towards taxes on exhaustible resources, that in addition produce heavy damages to the environment when used for combustion, was intended to represent a first step for shaping a more efficient taxation system (with less deadweight-loss), at the same time more environmentally friendly and supportive of sustainable development.

It was explicitly stated in the Proposal that the tax would only be implemented once measures with an analogous financial impact were introduced by the other OECD countries. This conditionality clause could be spelt out as a way for putting pressure on the main countries competing in trade with European firms and especially on US and Japan, so that similar policies for limiting carbon dioxide emissions would be carried out at least at the level of the industrialised world. In the Commission's view it was also essential to avoid any deterioration of the competitive position – and the subsequent delocalisation of European firms – towards countries outside the OECD area implementing less stringent environmental standards, in particular for those industrial sectors employing energy intensive production processes and with a large involvement in international trade (steel, chemicals, non-ferrous, cement, glass, pulp and paper). A special fiscal treatment was provided, but the affected industries would be obliged to assume an engagement to voluntarily reduce CO_2 emissions.

4. From the carbon-energy tax proposal to the Emissions Trading System

Economists increasingly agree that, in defining the best policy option to control global warming and fight climate change, economic instruments permit the goal of curbing greenhouse gas emissions to be achieved at a lower cost than standards and regulations. However, a choice should be made between price instruments, such as a carbon tax, and quantity instruments, such as emission permits. "...In an environment of complete knowledge and perfect certainty there is a formal identity between the use of prices and quantities as planning instruments...". This is the basic assumption of the classical approach that goes back to Weitzman.[164] However, since asymmetric information is the rule and not the exception, a choice must be made.

164 M.L. Weitzman, "Prices vs. Quantities", in *The Review of Economic Studies*, October 1974, pp. 477-491.

In 1992, in preparation for the United Nations Conference on Environment and Development to be held in Rio, the European Community put forward a Draft Directive introducing a carbon-energy tax,[165] with the double goal of promoting energy-saving through the share of the tax linked to the quantity of energy used and fuel-switching through the tax rate linked to the carbon content of each fossil fuel.[166] However, after the failed attempt to introduce a carbon-energy tax, the EU Council decided to follow a different path and finally approved a Directive[167] introducing an Emissions Trading System (ETS).[168]

The ETS adopts a cap-and-trade method. The overall volume of greenhouse gases that can be emitted each year by the power plants, factories and other companies covered by the system is subject to the cap set at the EU level that, from 2013 onwards, is reduced by 1.74% each year. Within the Europe-wide cap, companies receive or buy emission allowances which they can trade. The number of allowances to be allocated and to whom was left to be decided through National Allocations Plans since there were differences between Member States' commitments under the EU burden-sharing agreement and the Kyoto Protocol. The activities covered are all combustion installations with a rated thermal input exceeding 20 MW: mineral oil refineries, coke ovens, production and processing of ferrous metals, mineral industry (cement, glass, ceramic products), production of pulp and paper, for a total of nearly 11,000 installations, representing about 45% of total emissions.

The allocation of permits takes place before the trading period begins, since ETS requires that polluters hold an entitlement to emit a given quantity of pollution, and covers carbon dioxide emissions from installations listed in Annex 1 of the Directive. Each allowance gives the holder the right to emit one tonne of CO_2. Allowances can be used only once since companies have to surrender allowances for every tonne of CO_2 that they emitted in the previous year.

For the first three years the allowances to participating installations were allocated for free, with the possibility of auctioning up to 5% of

---

165 The Draft Directive on carbon-energy tax was presented by the Commission on June 1992, but it was never approved by the Council.

166 A. Majocchi, "The Rationale behind Energy Taxation. The European Commission's Proposal of an Energy-Carbon Tax", in IFA, *Environmental Taxes and Charges*, Florence, 1993, pp. 27-44.

167 European Commission, *Directive 2003/87/EC establishing a scheme for greenhouse gas emissions allowance trading within the Community*, 13 October 2003.

168 J. Delbeke, *EU Energy Law*, Claeys & Casteels, Leuven, 2006.

allowances. For the five-year period beginning in January 2008, Member States allocated at least 90% of the allowances free of charge (Article 10), while "...further harmonisation of the method of allocation was foreseen...", including a progressive shift towards the auctioning of allowances in place of cost-free allocation for the third trading period 2013-2020 (Article 30(2)(c) of the Directive). Therefore, whereas the vast majority of emission allowances was previously given free by governments, from 2013 auctioning became the main method of allocating them, according to the principle that the polluter pays. But the experience of power generators, which from 2013 had to buy their allowances, shows that they have been able to pass on the notional cost of allowances to customers, thus avoiding being charged the costs of the uneconomic externalities their production entails.

The possession of allowances entitles operators to emit greenhouse gases, and allowances can be transferred between persons within the EU. By 30 April each year at the latest, the operator of each installation must surrender a number of allowances equal to the total emissions from that installation during the preceding calendar year and these allowances will be subsequently cancelled (Article 12(c) of the Directive 87/2003). Heavy fines are imposed if they do not surrender enough allowances to match their emissions.

5. Limits of the Kyoto Agreement on curbing CO_2 emissions

A worldwide agreement on curbing CO_2 emissions was reached on 11 December 1997 at the Conference of Parties (COP3) that took place in Kyoto.[169] The approach adopted at Kyoto entails that each country limits the quantity of its emissions so that the global emissions reduction target may be achieved. However, the Kyoto approach has one significant weakness: it is based on emissions measured according to the level of production, not consumption. If a country delocalises energy-intensive industrial production towards other areas where labour costs are lower, while importing the same goods from these countries, then carbon production in that country has been cut, but not consumption.

[169] The Kyoto Protocol is an international agreement linked to the United Nations Framework Convention on Climate Change, which commits its Parties by setting internationally binding emission reduction targets.

The UK is an example of switching production while maintaining high consumption: British carbon production went down by over 15% between 1990 and 2005 since the UK de-industrialised and switched from coal to gas to generate electricity. However, if carbon consumption is measured adding to production carbon imports – and aviation and shipping – we find that the UK's emissions went up by around 19%. The conclusion is quite straightforward: "...much of the emissions in China are for us, not the Chinese. The emissions are produced in China, to be consumed in Europe and the US [...]. We should pay for our emissions wherever they are produced...".[170]

The Kyoto agreement contains an incentive for energy-intensive sectors to switch production from capped countries to other uncapped countries, then to import the foreign goods for domestic consumption. This has a strong impact on the choice of the most effective instrument to move towards climate change mitigation. The system of permits is only effective if all major CO_2 producing countries are capped. However, if this is not the case, a leakage problem arises that could be solved by implementing a carbon tax based on emissions linked to domestic consumption, regardless of where the emissions are produced. This means that imported goods should be taxed in the same way as national products. In the absence of a similar measure, i.e. without a border tax adjustment (BTA), a cap-and-trade system could be counterproductive from an environmental point of view. In the case of the displacement of production abroad, carbon leakage refers to the amount of emissions reduction when domestic production falls in relation to the amount of carbon emitted in the areas of the world where production goes up. Hence, the displacement of production could lead to an increase in overall emissions if the carbon intensity of production abroad is much higher than at home.

According to Gros and Egenhofer,[171] "...a key parameter in any judgement of the efficiency of the ETS is thus the difference in energy and carbon intensity between the EU and its major trading partners...". In the literature,[172] it is estimated that every $1,000 of exports from China contains about 2-3 tonnes of carbon, which is about four/five times more

---

170 D.R. Helm, R. Smale, J. Philipps, *Too Good to Be True? The UK's Climate Change Record*, Oxford, New College, 10 December 2007.

171 D. Gros, C. Egenhofer, *Climate Change and Trade. Taxing Carbon at the Border?*, Brussels, Centre for European Policy Studies, 2010, p. 33.

172 G. Peters, E. Hertwich, E., "CO_2 Embodied in International Trade with Implications for Global Climate Policy", in *Environmental Science and Technology*, 2008, pp. 1401-1407.

than the 0.5 tonnes of carbon embodied in $1,000 of exports from the EU. If the carbon intensity of GDP is the issue, it appears that it is ten times higher in Russia than in the EU and six times higher in China. If it is agreed that as a benchmark Chinese production is generally about 4 to 5 times as carbon-intensive as that of the EU, it follows that the ETS might lead to an increase in global emissions if production leakage is somewhat above 20-25%.

There is another compelling argument in favour of complementing the cap-and-trade system with a carbon tax. To reach the necessary CO_2 emissions reduction goal, a floor price for permits should be guaranteed at the level needed to underpin low carbon investments. This outcome is not easy to achieve, as governments would have to intervene in the market by buying back permits to hold up the price. However, this behaviour implies a loss of revenue for treasuries that are already constrained by the SGP's rules. The implementation of a carbon tax, with a rate proportional to the carbon content of each energy source, would send a strong signal to the market of the determination to guarantee a carbon price floor. Contrary to what happens with grandfathered permits, the carbon tax, considered as a complement to the ETS, would provide new revenues that could be used to fund required investments, or to cut down other distortionary taxes, opening up the way to the achievement of a double dividend, at least in the weak version.[173]

6. A proposed revision of taxation of energy products

In 2011 the European Commission proposed an important revision of the Energy Taxation Directive 2003/96/EC, intended to address the problem of climate change by introducing a CO_2 element into energy taxation.[174] Energy consumption is responsible for a large part of greenhouse gas emission, representing 79% of total gas emissions.[175] Rational energy taxation could contribute in a technology-neutral way to cleaner and more efficient energy consumption. In this perspective, the new Directive, based on energy content and CO_2 emissions, aimed at rebalancing the charge

[173] A.L. Bovenberg, L.H. Goulder, *Environmental Taxation and Regulation*, NBER Working Paper 8458, Cambridge MA, September 2001.

[174] European Commission, *Proposal for a Council Directive amending Directive 2003/96/EC restructuring the Community framework for the taxation of energy products and electricity*, COM(2011) 169 final, Brussels, 13 April 2011.

[175] European Commission, *Smarter energy taxation for the EU: proposal for a revision of the Energy Taxation Directive*, COM(2011) 168/3, Brussels, 2011.

between different fuels, including renewable energies, and at putting a price on CO_2 emissions which are not covered by the ETS.

The proposal was not designed to raise additional revenue, but at targeting new resources to improve the fiscal structure. A growth-friendly tax shift, using additional revenue wholly or partly to cut down the tax burden on labour, or to provide incentives to green research and development as well as green investment, would be in line with this objective. Additional revenue could also be used to mitigate the impact on household incomes by compensating less well-off sections of the population: lump-sum subsidies, unrelated to energy consumption, to low income households could help achieve this target.

In the proposal taxes on energy would be split into two parts: one based on CO_2 content and the other based on energy content. A single minimum rate for CO_2 emissions of the energy product (€20 per tonne CO_2) would be introduced for all sectors not covered by the ETS, thus providing a carbon price for households, transport, smaller business and agriculture, all sector now outside the ETS.[176] Emitters included in ETS will be exempt from the CO_2 part of taxation. Renewable energy sources that comply with the sustainability criteria laid down in Article 17 of Directive 2009/28/EC would not be subject to this CO_2 element. Tax rates for energy would be based on the energy content of a fuel measured in Gigajoules (GJ), since a fuel will be taxed with a minimum rate of €0.15/GJ on the basis of the amount of energy that it generates: one GJ will be taxed in the same way regardless of the product generating it (motor fuels, heating fuels, electricity).

Both CO_2 and energy content could be combined to define the overall rate at which a product is taxed. These are considered as minimum rates, that means that Member States will be free to raise the rate above this minimum level, but the same rates and structure must then be applied to all fuels used for the same purpose. Differentiation between private and commercial use of transport would no longer continue, ensuring that the transport sector – the fastest growing source of emissions – was not left outside the emission reduction effort. A long transitional period was foreseen, up to 2023, to give time for industry to adapt to the new tax structure.

According to the Commission, this revised Energy Taxation Directive was designed to complement the third phase of the ETS (2013-2020),

---

176 For petrol, since 1000 litres emit 2.30 tCO_2, with a CO_2 price of €20 per tonne, the tax will amount to €46 or, for each litre, €0.046.

which will set forth an EU global cap and provide for the move from free allowances to the auctioning of permits. From an internal market perspective, it is important to adopt a common framework for CO_2 taxation to avoid Member States approaches differing too much, hence providing new obstacles to fair competition within the internal market. Finally, given that Member States were at that time defining their policy strategies to emerge from the economic and financial crisis, this revised Energy Directive could provide an opportunity to match environmental and economic targets, shifting some of the tax burden away from labour or capital and towards taxation that promotes environmentally-friendly, energy-efficient behaviours.

The proposal addressed the problem of carbon leakages, introducing an approach similar to the free allowances under the ETS for sectors that are deemed to be at significant risk of leaving Europe following the new tax burden. In order to maintain full incentives to reduce emissions and guarantee the environmental effect of the tax, while compensating companies, small industrial installations subject to CO_2-related taxation would be granted a lump sum tax credit calculated on the basis of the historic energy consumption of the installation concerned in a specified reference period. The amount of the tax credit would reflect the CO_2 tax that would have been incurred on the basis of the historic consumption figures under the assumption that a CO_2-efficient reference fuel had been used. For the purpose of this fuel benchmark, the emission factor of natural gas would be used.

The impact of the new Directive would be dependent to a large degree on choices made by Member States in accordance with the subsidiarity principle. For instance, for heating fuels two alternative scenarios have been imagined: a) Member States decide to introduce CO_2-related taxation equal to the minimum level of €20 per tonne CO_2 on top of their existing national tax rates. In this case, the change in annual tax revenue will be €39.6 billion, with a 4% reduction of CO_2 emissions in non-ETS sectors by 2020 and a 0.29% increase in households' real income; b) Member States revise their tax rates only if needed to respect the EU minima, while fixing the CO_2-related taxation at €20 per tonne CO_2. The revenue would be lower (€20 billion) with a 0.84% reduction in CO_2 emissions in non-ETS sectors, while households' real income will remain practically stable (+ 0.08%). According to the assessment of the Commission services, the positive environmental impact could be represented by a cut of 2% of total EU emissions, corresponding to 92mt CO_2 that represents about 37% of the greenhouse gases reduction effort outside the ETS sectors. The positive impact on employment would reach one million new jobs in 2030, following the additional economic growth driven by the assumption that additional revenue from energy taxation would be used to cut down employers' social security contributions.

This proposal too was never approved by the Council and was finally retired by the Commission in 2015. But some conclusions can be drawn from this experience. First, within the European Union the idea seems to be emerging that it is necessary to move in the direction of addressing the problem of global warming using both quantity and price economic instruments, *i.e.* that the ETS should be complemented by a carbon-energy tax. The proportion of the carbon element of the tax should be adjusted in parallel to the market price of the permits, while the proportion of the energy element would be adjusted to keep the value stable in real terms. This point is relevant: investments targeted at the production of new clean energy sources need guarantees of stability over time of the tax component in the price of fossil fuels. Second, economic instruments for fighting climate changes would be used in all the sectors of the economy, while now only a part of emissions is subject to the ETS. This enlargement would increase the effectiveness of the policy for curbing CO_2 emissions. Third, the support for renewable energy sources should be guaranteed through the market, as all fossil fuels in different uses will be charged according to the relative carbon (and energy) content. The incentive for the production of carbon-free energy sources will be automatically linked to the tax to be paid on fuels with high carbon content. Fourth, the tax will provide a revenue that could be used for different purposes: promoting green investments, reducing the tax burden on labour through a reduction of social security contributions or limiting the regressivity of energy taxation through the lowering of tax burden on low income families. In this way the possibility of enjoying a double dividend is increased.

7. Carbon tax and border tax adjustments

Given the dramatic urgency that the problem of climate changes presents, the idea of introducing a carbon tax, as a complement to the Emissions Trading System (ETS), to act as an instrument to control carbon dioxide emissions and to comply with the commitments assumed by the European Union at the COP 21 (Conference of Parties) in Paris,[177] is

[177] The COP21, that has taken place from 30 November to 12 December 2015, has negotiated, with the consent of the 195 Parties involved, the Paris Agreement on curbing greenhouse gases, that foresees as its objective to limit the increase in global

now back on the political agenda. This tax should necessarily be defined according to a common scheme to avoid distortions in the European energy market, even if it is possible to conceive that the revenue is distributed between the European and the national tier of government, so that Member States can remove the regressive impact of the carbon tax, favouring most deprived families through adequate fiscal reductions in income taxation.

French President Emmanuel Macron's speech, given at La Sorbonne University in Paris, proposing an *Initiative for a sovereign, united, democratic Europe*,[178] put forward many new ideas. In view of the upcoming negotiations on the next Multiannual Financial Framework 2021-2027, the most significant suggestion emerging from his speech concerned the resources to be allocated to finance the European budget. Here, particular emphasis was made on the role of a carbon tax. This was considered as the price to be paid for using fuels that during the combustion process emit carbon dioxide and pollute the environment, increasing the risks of climate change. From this point of view, the carbon tax could be considered as the price to be paid not only to compensate for the damage caused by polluting a common good, but also – and this is the other side of the coin – to purchase the *permit* to (legally) release the (residual) greenhouse gases into the atmosphere. Then, to a certain degree, the carbon tax could be seen as a way for *getting prices right* similar to the emission allowances that are the cornerstone of the Emissions Trading Scheme adopted by the European Union. On the market, prices cover all monetary costs, but do not include the costs for using environmental resources. Carbon pricing, putting a price on the use of carbon, is a way to provide an efficient answer to this market failure.

According to Macron, the levying of a carbon tax could be politically feasible only if "…the European firms that are more involved in the globalisation process are put on a level playing field with the competing foreign firms that are working in countries with less stringent environmental constraints. For this reason, a border tax on carbon is unavoidable…". This idea represents the only way to reach a consensus

warming to less than 2 degrees Celsius (°C) with regard to the level of the pre-industrial phase. The European Union has fixed initially the goal to cut down at least of 20% the emission of greenhouse gases before 2020 with regard to 1990. In October 2014 the objective has been raised to a 40% reduction before 2030 and 85-90% reduction before 2050, if the other industrialised countries will engage in pursuing the same objective.

178 *Initiative pour l'Europe*. Discours d'Emmanuel Macron: *Pour une Europe souveraine, unie, démocratique*, Paris, 26 Septembre 2017.

on carbon pricing, since it allows for problems of carbon leakage and loss of competitiveness of European production to be avoided, while facilitating the transition towards a new model of sustainable growth. In the meantime, the implementation of border tax adjustments (BTA) is highly controversial, both from an economic point of view and in terms of compatibility with WTO rules. Hence, it is important to show that the combination of BTA and a carbon tax is a welfare-enhancing measure and could be structured so that it is consistent with the principles governing international trade relations.

8. A carbon tax for financing the EU budget

A carbon tax can be considered as the best instrument for *getting prices right*, correcting the negative externality linked to the pollution engendered by carbon dioxide emissions deriving from combustion of fossil fuels, and thus curbing the use of polluting energy sources and favouring the achievement of the Kyoto targets. At the same time, a carbon tax could provide a large amount of revenue to finance the expenditures essential for facing the challenges with which the European Union is actually confronted.

The taxable base of the carbon tax should not include sectors that are already part of the ETS, whose allowances will be progressively allocated through an auctioning mechanism – as a step by step abolition of the free allocation of allowances – with an additional revenue that, according to the conclusion of the Monti Report should be attributed to the EU budget. The revenue collected through the auctioning of allowances could probably reach an amount around €15-20 billion.[179]

---

[179] In 2015 emission in sectors included in the ETS amount to 1,305 million tonnes (source Eurostat). With a price for emission allowances that is increasing from the beginning of 2018 and has already risen above €21, the revenue collected through the auctioning of ETS allowances and allocated to the EU27 budget could amount to around 27.5 billion. This evaluation could be checked with another one, considering that the amount of emissions could have diminished from 2015 up to now. Since the Commission has proposed to allocate 20% of the money collected through the auctioning of ETS allowances to the EU budget, with a forecast of the amount flowing to the budget varying between €1.2 and 3 billion (European Commission, *Proposal for a Council Decision on the System of Own resources of the European Union*, COM(2018) 325final, Brussels, 2 May 2018), if all the receipts deriving from the auctioning of the ETS allowances will attributed to the EU budget, they could reach an amount between €6 and 15 billion.

According to Eurostat, in the EU27 emissions of carbon dioxide in sectors not included in ETS amount in 2016 to 2,216.34mt. So, with a rate of €50[180] for each tonne of CO_2 emitted,[181] the carbon tax could provide a revenue of around €110.8 billion,[182] that would represent around 75% of the current size of the EU budget (in 2018 the appropriations foreseen in the Draft General Budget reach around €145 billion). Since a barrel of oil is equivalent to about 159 litres and emits 0.366 tonnes of CO_2, the emission of a CO_2 tonne derives from the use of 2.7 barrels, or 429 litres. The increase in the cost of a litre of gasoline, with a rate of €50 for each tonne of CO_2, and supposing a current gasoline price equal to €1.5, will be equal to €0.116, an increase approaching 7.7%.

An effective design of carbon tax – introduced as a complement to the Emission Trading System within the European Union – should include a tax levied on carbon consumption, therefore including the taxation of imports of energy-intensive goods. This implies that the carbon tax should combine a domestic proxy for consumption and a border tax adjustment. The existing ETS covers less than half of total carbon emissions, since buildings and the domestic sector are not covered, and much of the transport sector is excluded along with agriculture. The new carbon tax could be a fuel tax levied on coal, gas and oil weighted according to their carbon content and, to the extent that consumption is targeted by its carbon inputs, is a proxy for a carbon consumption tax.

180 In the *Report of the High-Level Commission on Carbon Prices*, (www.carbonpricing leadership.org), published in 2017 by a group of experts chaired by J.E. Stiglitz and N. Stern on behalf of Ségolène Royal and Feike Sijbesma, co-chairs of the *Carbon Pricing Leadership Coalition High-Level Assembly*, the conclusion is reached that "… the explicit carbon-price level consistent with achieving the Paris temperature target is at least US$40-80 by 2020 and US$50-100 by 2030, provided a supportive policy-environment is in place…". These prices, at the current rate of exchange, are equivalent to a minimum price varying between €34 – €68 in 2020 and €42,5 – €85 in 2030. Therefore, a rate equal to €50 falls within the average of this range.

181 To avoid political problems and for efficiency reasons it could seem reasonable to foresee gradualism in the introduction of the tax, with an initial rate sufficiently high to provide a restriction in consumption behavior of families and firms, while it will increase in due time to reach the level of €50 for each tCO_2. In this way it will be possible to adapt progressively the structure of fossil fuels consumption given the price differential following the implementation of the carbon tax. The final rate could also follow the development of the goals pursued by the Union as far as the curbing of CO_2 emissions is concerned.

182 If the rate suggested in the Macron's speech of €25-30 euro for each of CO_2 emitted will be initially adopted, the revenue will amount respectively to €55.5 and €66.5 billion.

The domestic tax should be complemented by a border tax adjustment (BTA) levied on imports of goods coming from countries that do not put a price on carbon,[183] so that the competitiveness of European firms is not impaired and the risk of carbon leakage controlled, while respecting the WTO rules. This choice is fundamental to guarantee the political acceptability of taxing carbon within the EU, as a BTA will prevent damaging distortions in European production. However, the adoption of BTA remains controversial as it is sometimes rejected as contrary to WTO rules. It does not seem that a level playing field is excluded by fair competition at the international level. But what is more important is to underline that a BTA is essential to prevent the risk of a loss of competitiveness for domestic firms that could make the adoption of such a tax difficult.

CO_2 emissions deriving from production processes within the EU28 amount to 5.6 tonnes CO_2 *per capita* (source Eurostat). Of these, "…a smaller part, equal to 1.1 tonnes/person, is estimated to have originated from production activities outside the EU28 that created intermediate and final products that were then imported into the EU28 for final use…". Given these per capita emissions incorporated in products coming from outside the Union and given the total population living in the EU, equal to 441 million, total emissions *imported* will amount to 485 mt CO_2. With a tax paid at the borders of the Union, equal to the domestic carbon tax paid within the EU, an additional revenue will flow to the European budget equal to €24 billion. If this revenue were added to the receipts flowing from domestic carbon tax with a rate of €50 per tonne CO_2 (€110.8 billion) and to the revenue deriving from the auctioning of allowances in the ETS (varying between €15 and €20 billion), a grand total of around €150 billion could be reached.

The concept underlying a BTA is the destination principle, according to which goods are taxed where they are consumed, not where they are produced. The border charge on imports should be equivalent to the tax on the corresponding domestic product since, according to the WTO rules, a state shall not discriminate between domestic and foreign goods. Even if a BTA were considered a border enforcement of EU domestic tax, it cannot treat imported products less favourably than *like* domestic

183 D. Gros, C. Egenhofer, *Climate Change and Trade. Taxing carbon at the border?*, CEPS, Brussels, 2010. On the compatibility with WTO rules: A. Majocchi, "Carbon-energy tax, emission permits and border tax adjustments", in L. Kreiser (ed.), *Carbon Pricing, Growth and the Environment*, Edwar Elgar, 2012, pp. 230-243; J. Hillman, *Changing Climate for Carbon Taxes. Who's Afraid of the WTO?*, The German Marshall Fund of the United States, Climate and Energy Paper Series, Washington, July 2013.

products. But, basing the tax on the carbon content of the imported goods makes sure that a BTA is compatible with Article I, according to which the EU cannot discriminate against an import based on its *origin*.

9. Carbon tax and the Energy and Environment Agency

The introduction of a carbon tax – that has received the support of the French President, but has also been discussed in the Monti Report and in the Commission's Reflection Paper[184] – should be complemented by the creation of an Energy and Environment Agency (EEA), to be set up during processes of revision of the Euratom Treaty.[185] Within the Agency, the carbon tax could play a similar role to that foreseen in the Coal and Steel Community, where Article 49 authorised a levy on the production of coal and steel, with a rate not higher – except with a special derogation by a majority equal to 2/3 in the Council – than 1% of the average value of each product and targeted at financing a restructuring of production in these sectors.

Equally, the carbon tax could be conceived of not only as an instrument to correct a negative externality deriving from the consumption of fossil fuels, but also as a levy that would be collected at the national level according to common European rules. The receipts could be utilised, at least partially, as a contribution to the EEA to support research and production in the renewable energy sector and, at the same time, to promote the deep structural changes; these follow necessarily from reducing traditional production, linked to the use of fossil fuels, and from the gradual disappearance of the nuclear sector.

---

[184] *Future Financing of the EU*, Final Report and Recommendations of the High Level Group on Own Resources (Mario Monti Chairman), Brussels, December 2016; European Commission, *Reflection Paper on the Future of EU Finances*, Brussels, 28 June 2017.

[185] In the *Roadmap for a More United and More Democratic Union (Draft Commission Work Programme up to the end 2018)*, among the initiatives to be launched with a 2025 perspective, it is foreseen a "Communication on the future of EU energy and climate policy, including on the future of the Euratom Treaty (taking account of Declaration n. 54 of five Member States added to the Final Act of the Treaty of Lisbon and on the possible use of Article 192(2) second subparagraph TFEU". The Declaration No. 54 stated that "Germany, Ireland, Hungary, Austria and Sweden note that the core provisions of the Treaty establishing the European Atomic Energy Community have not been substantially amended since its entry into force and need to be brought up to date. They therefore support the idea of a Conference of the Representatives of the Governments of the Member States, which should be convened as soon as possible".

Furthermore, revenue flowing from the carbon tax could be used to favour the restructuring of the workforce currently employed in declining sectors of the economy, or to promote the employment of unskilled labour, through a reduction of social security contributions paid for these workers, according to the scheme of a double dividend foreseen in the Delors White Paper.[186] In reality, the introduction of the new levy should have two objectives. The first, ensuring a European contribution to curbing carbon dioxide emissions and favouring the control of the risks of climate change, that cannot be guaranteed by national policies. The second, supporting the restructuring of declining economic sectors – energy-intensive industries, production and distribution of by-products of fossil fuels, nuclear sector that is destined to a progressive contraction – in favour of the enlarging sectors, that is the production of renewable energy sources.

So, the substantial revenues deriving from putting a price on carbon could be directed in three different directions. The first part, coming from taxation of imports at the border, could flow directly to the Union's budget, to finance European public goods whose production is necessary to promote a new model of sustainable growth[187] that will gradually emerge within Europe (research and innovation, new technologies, environmental protection, education and new skills, health care and support for the deprived sectors of the population), and to support the first initiatives aiming at the implementation of a policy targeted to providing internal and external security (control of external borders, integration of migrants, defence).

A second share of the revenue would be treated as national contributions towards financing the Energy and Environment Agency, whose main task should be the provision of investments, domestically and in African countries, designed to support a transition to a free-carbon economy. This means that new money could be employed for funding the Juncker Plan and the External Investment Plan, improving competitiveness of

---

186 European Commission, *Growth, Competitiveness, Employment. The Challenges and Ways Forward into the 21st Century*, White Paper, COM(93) 700, Brussels, 5 December 1993.

187 At the Social Summit held in Gothenburg on 17 November 2017 the European Parliament, the Council and the European Commission jointly proclaimed the European Pillar of Social Rights, which was first announced by President Juncker in his 2015 State of the Union Address. The achievement of these goals should be included in a model of sustainable development. A step in this direction is represented by L. Fransen, G. del Bufalo, E. Reviglio, *Boosting Investments in social infrastructure in Europe*, Report of the High-level Task Force on investing in Social Infrastructure in Europe chaired by R. Prodi and C. Sautter, Discussion Paper 074, Brussels, 23 January 2018.

European firms with the provision of clean, cheap, renewable and secure energy sources and supporting a Marshall Plan for Africa that will finally provide the basis for an effective policy on controlling migration flows.

A third part of the revenue could remain in the hands of Member States. It is generally assumed that energy taxation is regressive. This is only partially true,[188] but it is reasonable that some tax relief in the field of income taxation should be ring-fenced for poor families, where the share of energy costs of income is higher than average. At the same time, the same tax relief could be provided, for a limited period, to energy-intensive firms, if they commit themselves to moving rapidly along the path towards a radical change in their pattern of energy consumption.

A final advantage of carbon taxation comes from the chance it gives to promote the consumption of renewable energy through the difference in tax payments towards fossil fuels, thus avoiding the use of administrative regulations or subsidies at the national level, that put a heavy burden on firms and families and substantially distort fair competition in the energy markets. Renewable energies' competitiveness would increase naturally, alongside a growth in production, following the increase in demand for these cheaper sources of energy, but in any case, the fiscal differential towards fossil fuels remain justified from the need to internalise the negative externalities linked to the polluting emissions of traditional energy.

188 K. Kosonen, "Regressivity of environmental taxation: myth or reality?", in J.E. Milne, M.S. Andersen (eds.), *Handook of Research on Environmental Taxation*, Edward Elgar, 2012, pp. 161-174.

Chapter 8

Carbon leakage and border tax adjustments

1. The relation between trade rules and environmental protection

The relation between trade and environment is acquiring high priority on the political agenda. The discussion is no longer confined to specialised bodies like the World Trade Organisation, but now involves a larger public. The reason is quite simple. From one side, with a higher level of income, demand for environmental goods is increasing rapidly, especially in the industrialised world. Until now, environmental protection has been carried out mainly through command-and-control measures. Regulations have been issued, that are normally different from one country to another. New obstacles to trade could thus derive from the need to comply with different standards in different countries. Over the last few years, economic instruments have been used more and more as a useful tool for internalising external environmental costs. However, the use of charges or taxes raises new problems, especially over reductions in external competitiveness for countries where new burdens are levied on industrial sectors, putting them at a comparative disadvantage over competitors in countries where the level of environmental protection is less constraining.

Another major change that has come about in the field of environmental policy can explain renewed interest in the issue. While first-generation environmental protection measures overwhelmingly addressed domestic environmental problems, the world has now assumed a fresh consciousness of the urgency of global problems, whereby all mankind, including future generations, is involved. It is easily understandable that a further difficulty is presented by these global problems: purely domestic measures are by definition inadequate to cope with these kind of problems and free-rider behaviour can be predicted from countries that try to win a competitive advantage, while enjoying the benefits flowing from common efforts. Consequently, environmental goals appear more difficult to achieve and large trade distortions can arise.

There are three main issues that should be dealt with when developing a sound policy on relations between trade and environment:

- trade liberalisation: world trade suggests that there is no contradiction at all between trade expansion and environmental protection. Trade liberalisation is a *good* per se, since it promotes economic growth and consequently provides more income that could be devoted to the conservation of the environment;
- unilateral trade restrictions for environmental purposes: some environmental groups assume that environmental policy is in all cases a priority over trade concerns. Consequently, unilateral trade measures with extra-jurisdictional effects could also be utilised without any constraints to promote the fulfilment of environmental goals;
- market access: industrialised countries have, up to now, been mainly responsible for the depletion of natural resources and for the deterioration of the global environment. These now have to provide a positive answer to the worries of developing countries, which greatly fear that their growth possibilities will be limited by stringent environmental standards tailored to the needs of the more advanced countries.

It is certainly true that trade liberalisation generally enhances social welfare, but this may not represent a sufficient condition if important distortions remain in the market. From an environmental standpoint the most significant of these is produced in cases where environmental costs are not internalised; this is a very wide deviation from efficiency conditions, since prices do not correctly reflect the resource costs of the goods.

Therefore, even if liberalisation of trade is one very important efficiency condition that should be pursued as far as possible, its implementation should at least be constrained by policy measures aiming at internalising the costs of environmental resources. As a matter of fact, the answer to the question of whether increased liberalisation of world trade is compatible with the goal of long-term sustainable development depends on the extent and the speed at which environmental effects are internalised. If environmental effects are not controlled, an expanding world economy will in the long run be incompatible with conservation of the ecosystem and, therefore, threaten the very basis for life on earth. Therefore, the idea of *getting the prices right* should be rightly considered as the best way for promoting sustainable development.

An example of the validity of this principle could easily be derived in the field of energy. If trade were totally liberalised and existing world market fragmentation was overcome, a drop in prices and an ensuing increase in demand, for energy as well, would result from enhanced competition, with a negative environmental impact (*e.g.* acid rain, atmospheric pollution, global warming *etc.*). Past experience has shown a clear relationship between the price of energy and the amount of carbon dioxide emissions, especially in the transport sector. These emissions have generally increased in parallel with GDP, but when oil prices have plunged, emissions rose faster than GDP. These negative effects could be avoided if trade liberalisation were backed up by an internalisation of the external costs of energy, for instance through the implementation of a carbon tax that accounts for all the external costs linked to the use of energy.

The conclusion can thus be drawn that trade liberalisation only increases welfare if the constraint of a good environmental policy internalising external costs is fully complied with. This point was already clearly made in *Agenda 21*, approved at the Earth Summit in Rio in June 1992. Environment and trade policy should be mutually supportive. An open, multilateral trading system makes a more efficient allocation and use of resources possible. It thus provides additional resources needed for economic growth and development, and improved environmental protection. An open, multilateral trading system, supported by the adoption of sound environmental policies, would have a positive impact on the environment and contribute to sustainable development. But this compromise between trade and environment could be avoided only if adequate policy measures are implemented in the environmental field.

2. Domestic and global environmental goods

In the design of an effective policy a clear distinction should be drawn between different types of environmental goods, and chiefly between domestic environmental goods, whose benefits are enjoyed mainly by people living within the borders of the country concerned by environmental policy decisions, and global environmental goods, whose benefits are enjoyed by all mankind or, at least, by people living in different countries. It is especially for these types of environmental goods that problems concerning trade might arise and compatible solutions should be defined.

For domestic environmental goods existing trade rules do not challenge at all the right of each country to introduce high standards of environmental protection. Each country can introduce stringent human, animal or plant life or health standards and has the sovereign right to tax or regulate imported products and similar domestic products as long as its taxes or regulations do not discriminate against imported products or afford protection to domestic producers. The European Union, as a unit, is now constrained, according to Article 191(2) TFEU, to seek high levels of environmental protection.

Problems arise when one has to deal with global environmental goods. In this case it seems reasonable to start from two very general principles:

- no country has the right to establish optimal environmental policy for the entire world. This principle sets a limit to unilateral decisions with extra-jurisdictional effects;
- but, in the case of global commons, it must be acknowledged that they do not belong to any particular country or to the present generation, but to the world as a whole and to the future generations as well.

A solution to this difficult paradox can be found through multilateral agreements establishing common rules for the sustainable management of global resources. No country can decide by itself on behalf of all the world, but at the same time no country should hamper the implementation of decisions taken on the basis of a multilateral consensus.

These principles already appeared in the 1992 Rio Declaration, that underlined the need of avoiding unilateral action to deal with environmental challenges outside the jurisdiction of the importing country. Thus, environmental measures addressing trans-border or global environmental problems should, as far as possible, be based on international consensus. While acknowledging that a multilateral approach is preferable, the Rio Declaration suggested that unilateral trade measures should be ruled out in principle, but some initiatives could be adopted according to the precautionary principle if:

- the process for reaching a multilateral agreement – that is likely to be time-consuming – has already started;
- a positive conclusion cannot be achieved due to the opposition of a particular country (or group of countries);
- there is a strong scientific evidence that reaching a general consensus for implementing urgent and unavoidable protection measures cannot wait. Even in this case, care should be taken to adopt the least trade-restrictive measures.

A further important point remains to be analysed. In many cases, the only real possibility of advancing towards a multilateral agreement in the case of global commons is to unilaterally implement domestic policy measures to incite other countries to adopt a similar policy. A good example was the proposal of the European Commission for limiting carbon dioxide emissions through a package of policy measures including an energy/carbon tax. One of the goals of this proposal was to push other industrialised countries so that they would pursue an effective policy targeted to switching to less carbon-intensive fuels and to improving energy efficiency.

Nonetheless, there may be significant drawbacks following a possible unilateral introduction of a carbon tax within the European Union, that is once again in the forefront of political debate after the endorsement of a carbon tax made by President Emmanuel Macron at the Sorbonne University. The most significant is that the tax could reduce competitiveness of European energy-intensive industries on the world market, thus also impairing the effectiveness of the policy for curbing carbon dioxide emissions. Here, the positive effects of the package of measures could be offset by a shift of international demand away from European industries, in favour of countries that implement no controls on carbon dioxide emissions and whose industries are more polluting but, at least in the short-run, more competitive.

3. Carbon leakages and external competitiveness

If global commons are at stake, attention should be given to the fact that states are interdependent. Hence, the effectiveness of the policy pursued by one state depends on what the other states do. This interdependence falls into two types. First, if one country curbs its emissions, this benefits other countries. But the country implementing emissions control does not receive any compensation for these benefits and therefore does not take them into account when setting its own levels of emission reductions. There should be a presumption that each group of countries will insufficiently reduce its emissions relative to the amount that would be justified from a global perspective. Free-riding therefore blocks the achievement of an effective environmental policy.

Second, following the adoption of strict environmental rules prices of traded goods would rise and, as a consequence, comparative advantage in the manufacture of these goods would shift abroad. As output of these goods rises abroad, emissions are likely to rise as well. These market effects are known as leakages that, if real and proven, undermine the environmental effectiveness of unilateral reduction policy.

In the literature, leakages are usually considered part of general competitiveness issues. Two types of negative effects are usually claimed in this context: eco-dumping and industrial migration to so-called pollution havens. Those concerned about eco-dumping argue that industries in countries with lower or unenforced environmental standards have a competitive advantage, while pollution havens cause industrial migration, resulting in jobs and foreign direct investment being diverted from countries with exacting standards to countries with lax ones. In particular, the conventional wisdom is that environmental regulations impose significant costs, slow productivity growth and thereby hinder the ability of domestic firms to compete on international markets. This loss of competitiveness is believed to be reflected in declining exports, increasing imports and a long-term movement of manufacturing capacity abroad, particularly in pollution-intensive industries.

Evidence of countries deliberately resorting to low environmental standards to gain competitive advantage or to attract investments does not seem available. No systematic competitive impacts from unequal environmental regulations, no significant loss of markets, domestically or abroad, due to eco-dumping, nor industrial migration to countries with lower environmental standards has been documented. It is generally recognised that environmental regulations do not normally engender large adverse effects on competitiveness, however that elusive term is defined. Although some long-run costs of environmental regulations cannot be excluded, it is difficult to find studies attempting to measure the effect of environmental regulation on net exports, overall trade flows, and plant-location decisions that have been able to produce estimates that are either large, statistically significant, or robust to tests of model specification.

There are different reasons why the effect of environmental regulation on competitiveness is small. For all but the most heavily regulated industries the cost of complying with environmental regulation is a relatively small share of total cost of production. Even where there are substantial differences between environmental requirements, within the internal market and abroad, domestic firms – and other multinationals as well – are reluctant to build below state-of-the-art plants in foreign countries. Finally, even in developing countries where environmental standards – and certainly enforcement capabilities – are relatively weak, new plants normally embody more pollution controls than are required. Therefore, even significant statutory differences in pollution control requirements between countries may not result in significant effects on plant location or other aspects of competitiveness. The main conclusion that can then be drawn is that cost differentials stemming from divergent environmental regulations do not pose sufficient threats to industrial competitiveness to justify substantial cutbacks in domestic environmental constraints.

Following the ideas initially put forward by Michael E. Porter,[189] environmental regulations have begun to be seen not only as benign in their impacts on international competitiveness, but actually as a net positive force driving private firms and the whole economy to become more competitive in international markets. Nonetheless, the current view remains that competitiveness might be reduced by the implementation of stringent environmental policy; this broadly accepted idea makes it more difficult to adopt new measures, especially when global – and not domestic – environmental goods are concerned by policy decisions.

Porter's argument is that strict environmental regulations can trigger innovation that may eventually raise a firm's competitiveness, outweighing any increased costs due to compliance with environmental rules. His argument has been supported by a large number of case studies showing examples of firms improving their economic performance following the implementation of tough environmental constraints.[190]

The basic idea is that these *innovation offsets* will be widespread, since reducing pollution often coincides with improving productivity in resource usage; hence, the external shock through environmental regulation may reduce existing X-inefficiencies and organisational failures within a firm, and may move it towards its production possibility frontier. In addition, Porter and van der Linde put forward an argument that firms may try to exploit a first-mover advantage by developing an environmental technology which can provide later a competitive advantage when other countries are induced to follow the same path of more stringent environmental regulations.

For policy-makers, this idea of a possible *win-win* option has been seen as manna from heaven, because it relieved them of the difficult trade-off between environmental and other economic targets. But economists remain a bit sceptical about this idea of a *free lunch* and support the need to implement a full cost-benefit analysis of environmental policy before reaching the conclusion that this policy is beneficial not only for

189 M.E. Porter, *The Competitive Advantage of Nations*, 1990, New York, Free Press.

190 M.E. Porter, C. Van der Linde, "Toward a New Conception of the Environment-Competitiveness Relationship", in *Journal of Economic Perspectives*, 1995, pp. 97-118.

the environment, but also for the economy as a whole. Two significant assumptions underlying the Porter and van der Linde perspective have been highlighted in particular: first, they see a private sector that systematically foregoes profit opportunities for innovation; secondly, they envisage a regulatory authority that is in a position to correct this market failure. But, even if the firm can invest and adopt new and more efficient technology, if that technology was not worth investing in before, its benefits would not be enough to raise the company's profits after the environmental standards are raised either.

In the literature, the validity of the Porter hypothesis has also been examined by considering firms' reactions with respect to both the type and the quantity of equipment in which they invest in response to changes in production costs, that trigger a restructuring of the capital stock in such a way that average productivity increases. If firms invest in machines of different ages, younger machines are more productive and less polluting than older ones, but are costlier to buy and to install in the capital stock. Environmental regulation accelerates the removal of older machines from the capital stock which increases its productivity. Thus, the implication that can be derived from the debate on the Porter hypothesis is not that a win-win situation can be expected, but that the trade-off between improving the environment and the competitiveness of the home industry is not as grim as it is sometimes suggested because of favourable changes in the composition of the capital stock.[191]

In any case, the prevailing view remains that competitiveness is reduced by the implementation of stringent environmental policy,[192] and this

---

191 "This paper has provided an overview of the key theoretical and empirical insights on the Porter Hypothesis to date. First, on the theoretical side, it turns out that the theoretical arguments that could justify the PH are now more solid than they appeared at first in the heated debate that took place in 1995 in the Journal of Economic Perspectives" (K. Palmer, W.E. Oates, P.R. Portney, "Tightening Environmental Standards: The Benefit-Cost or the No-Cost Paradigm?", in *Journal of Economic Perspectives*, 1995, pp. 119–132). On the empirical side, on one hand, the evidence about the *weak* version of the hypothesis (stricter regulation leads to more innovation) is also fairly well established. On the other hand, the empirical evidence on the strong version (stricter regulation enhances business performance) is mixed, with more recent studies providing more supportive results" (S. Ambec, M.A. Cohen, S. Elgie, P. Lanoie, *The Porter Hypothesis at 20: Can Environmental Regulation Enhance Innovation and Competitiveness?*, Resources for the Future Discussion Paper, 11/01, Washington, 2011).

192 "Significant relocation of energy-intensive industries away from the OECD may occur, depending on the type of market structure, with leakage rates as high as 130%, in which case GHG control policies in the industrialized countries actually lead to higher

widespread idea makes it more difficult to adopt new measures in policy decisions, especially when global – and not domestic – environmental goods are concerned. This was the case in recent years when the European Commission proposed the adoption of an energy/carbon tax that did not receive the support of the Council. Therefore, if, in facing increasing fears about the risks of climate change linked to fossil fuel consumption, the idea of a carbon tax has emerged again in the political debate, new instruments should be considered to avoid carbon leakages and loss of competitiveness for European firms. Recently, and for the first time, a political leader, French President Emmanuel Macron, clearly expressed his support for border tax adjustments, that imply the possibility of levying a countervailing duty on the price of imports coming from countries that do not put a price on the use of carbon. This seems to be the only realistic way out, and should be carefully taken into consideration.

4. The Rationale for Border Tax Adjustments

A well-designed carbon tax – introduced as a complement to the existing emissions trading system within the European Union – should take into account that the tax should be levied on carbon consumption, thus taxing imports of energy-intensive goods as well. This implies that the carbon tax should combine a domestic proxy for consumption and a border tax adjustment.[193] The existing ETS covers less than half of total carbon emissions, since buildings and domestic sector are not covered and much of the transport sector is excluded, as is the case for agriculture. The new carbon tax could be a fuel tax levied on coal, gas and oil, weighted according to their carbon content, and to the extent that consumption is targeted by its carbon inputs, it is a proxy for a carbon consumption tax.

This domestic tax should be complemented by a border tax adjustment (BTA). Since a global cap-and-trade system or a carbon tax encompassing all the major greenhouse gas emitters is at this stage unrealistic, a straightforward way to move towards a global level pricing of carbon would be for Europe to impose an import tax on the CO_2 content of all goods imported into the EU from countries that do not put a price on the use of carbon.

---

global emissions". (M.H. Babiker, "Climate change policy, market structure, and carbon leakage", in *Journal of International Economics*, March 2005, pp. 421-445).

193 "...A *border tax* is a tax (or customs duty) imposed on imported goods, while a *border tax adjustment* is an adjustment of the taxes imposed domestically on products when the goods are imported...". (WTO-UNEP, 2009).

This measure is extremely controversial since important administrative problems must be solved and it is sometimes rejected as contrary to WTO rules.[194] However, while a level playing field seems to be an important condition for fair competition at the international level, what is more important is that a BTA is essential to prevent domestic firms from risking a loss of competitiveness that could make it difficult to adopt such a tax (as already happened with the 1992 EC draft Directive), while an externality tax on a global public risk is undoubtedly an efficiency enhancing measure. As Gros and Egenhofer put it,[195] "…an import tariff improves global welfare because this transfers carbon pricing, at least partially, via trade flows, even to those parts of the world whose governments have so far refrained from imposing any domestic measures…". It remains to be seen whether a carbon border tax is compatible with WTO rules.

5. Border Tax Adjustments and WTO Rules

There are many reasonable arguments against taxing goods at borders. While the risk of increasing trade barriers should be ruled out – by carefully structuring European border tax adjustments so that they are compatible with WTO rules – putting a price on the use of fuels that emit carbon dioxide during combustion is a way to get prices right, since prices would include the costs of polluting the environment through the use – either domestically or abroad – of natural resources. However, taxing goods at the border according to their carbon content is also a prerequisite for the political acceptability of the carbon pricing proposal, ensuring that environmental protection does not significantly damage economic growth. Thus, one aspect of the proposal – putting a price on carbon – cannot be separated from the other – applying an import tax at the border on foreign products coming from countries with no price on carbon.

The BTA is based on the principle that goods are taxed where they are consumed, not where they are produced. Therefore, according to the GATT,[196] a border tax adjustment is defined as "…any fiscal measure

194 A. Majocchi, "Carbon-energy tax, emission permits and border tax adjustments", in L. Kreiser (ed.), *Carbon Pricing, Growth and the Environment*, Edwar Elgar, 2012, pp. 230-243; J. Hillman, *Changing Climate for Carbon Taxes. Who's Afraid of the WTO?*, The German Marshall Fund of the United States, Climate and Energy Paper Series, Washington, July 2013.

195 D. Gros, C. Egenhofer, *Climate Change and Trade. Taxing carbon at the border*, CEPS, Brussels, 2010, p. 38.

196 GATT Working Party Report, *Border Tax Adjustment*, L3464, 2 December 1970.

which puts into effect, in whole or in part, the destination principle…". There can be two types of BTAs: the levying of a tax on imported goods at the same level as domestic tax levied on similar goods (BTA on imports); the rebate of domestic taxes when goods are exported (BTA on exports). In the case of the ETS, the BTA could require that importers be obliged to purchase a number of permits corresponding to the quantity of emissions created during the manufacturing process of the imported goods.

There is a risk that the BTA could turn out to be a hidden trade barrier. The GATT Report on BTAs indicated that only indirect taxes could be eligible as border adjustments and that BTAs are compatible with existing rules if foreign and domestic goods are similar or like-products. In an Appellate Body's decision within the GATT,[197] the likeness of a product is defined according to four characteristics: the physical properties of the product; the ability of the product to serve the same or similar end-uses; the consumers' perception that a product could be considered as an alternative means to satisfy a particular want or demand; the international classification of products for tariff purposes.

The border charge on imports should be equivalent to the tax on the corresponding domestic product since, according to the WTO's rules, a State should not discriminate between domestic and foreign goods. The rules stipulate that the charge could be imposed through a measure equivalent to the internal tax "…in respect of the like domestic product or in respect of an article from which the imported product has been manufactured or produced in whole or in part…" (Article II.2a). This Article seems to reinforce the idea that the energy inputs and fossil fuels used in the production process could be considered to be such articles; it states that border tax adjustments are allowed in respect of the taxes applied *directly or indirectly* to like domestic products. Similarly, on exports, BTAs are considered as subsidies – and in this case are not admitted – only when they are levied *in excess* of taxes on like domestic products.

Even if a carbon border tax is considered a border enforcement of EU domestic tax, it cannot treat imported products less favourably than *like* domestic products. According to an Appellate Body's decision within the GATT,[198] two products are considered *like* if they are in a *competitive relationship*. Consequently, even if a basic industrial product is produced using two different production processes, one of which is more

---

[197] GATT, *Japan – Taxes on Alcoholic Beverages*, Report of the Appellate Body, WT/DS8, 10/11AB/R, 4 October 1996.

[198] GATT, *European Communities – Measures Affecting Asbestos and Products Containing Asbestos*, Report of the Appellate Body, WT/DS135/AB/R, March 2001.

carbon-intensive, they should be considered *like*. Hence, a carbon border adjustment, which is a tax on a *process* and not on a *product*, would infringe Article III.4, since it treats two *like* products differently. In this case, differentiation between *like products* is only permitted by invoking the General Exceptions. Trade-related measures are allowed under Article XX,[199] when they are needed to protect exhaustible resources or human, animal or plant life or health. A low-carbon atmosphere could reasonably be considered, since it is necessary to avoid catastrophic climate change, as an *exhaustible natural resource*.

Article III requires that imported goods should not be treated worse than domestic goods; therefore, the EU must be careful to impose a carbon BTA based on the carbon content of the import and that does not exceed domestic carbon tax. "…The rate of the tax should be equal to the difference between the EU price of carbon (€) and the foreign price of carbon. Hence, the tax on a product is going to be equal to the carbon content times the difference in the EU carbon price and foreign carbon price…".[200]

Basing the tax on the carbon content of the product ensures that a BTA will be compatible with Article I, according to which the EU cannot discriminate against an import based on its *origin*. The EU may argue that the BTA measure is not imposed based on origin, but on the production process. Therefore, one crucial detail in the implementation of the BTA is the methodology used to collect the information needed to determine the carbon footprint of each quantity of the imported good. This could be done, for example, by requiring imported products to be accompanied by certification or the labelling of the relevant aspects of their production process and related carbon emissions used in their production.[201] If export countries do not provide information about the production process, according to Gros and Egenhofer, the best solution (under WTO-compatibility considerations) would be to use an *external* standard, such as ISO 14067, to calculate the carbon footprint of imports.

---

199 P. Low, G. Marceau, J. Reinaud, *The Interface between the Trade and Climate Change Regimes: Scoping the Issues*, WTO, Staff Working Paper ERSD-2011-1, p. 487.

200 "…The border tax should tax the manufacturer or the importer at the point of the first sale or use of the imported product. The border tax should apply to all products as all products emit carbon during the production process…" (D. Gros, C. Egenhofer, *Climate Change and Trade. Taxing Carbon at the Border?*, Brussels, Centre for European Policy Studies 2010, p. 61).

201 J. Hillman, *ibidem*, p. 7.

6. Tax Exemptions and Border Tax Adjustments

The trade-off that seems to exist between environmental protection and external competitiveness is effectively one of the main hurdles to overcome in order to reach a political agreement to unilaterally implement domestic environmental protection measures, when global commons are at stake. In the long-run, sound environmental policy could improve domestic industrial structure, and thus also the competitive position of the country concerned, however, as, in the short term, external competitiveness seems to be impaired, it is much more difficult to get advanced environmental legislation adopted throughout the political process.

A way out of the dilemma between environmental effectiveness and external competitiveness was suggested in the proposal for a carbon/energy tax presented by the EU Commission.[202] This entailed the provision of tax exemptions for energy-intensive industries largely open to international trade, that "...are seriously disadvantaged on account of an imbalance in trade from other Member States or an increase in imports from third countries..." (Article 9:2). Since there are plenty of reasons to question the rationale behind this solution, it may be very important to ensure that a policy setting up a system of border tax adjustments to balance the cost differentials between domestic and foreign production due to the environmental tax is compatible with existing WTO rules.

If the adoption of an environmental tax is constrained by a conditionality clause, i.e. by the adoption of similar measures by other competing countries, this implies that deciding to unilaterally implement the environmental policy is out of the question, while it will still be extremely difficult to achieve multilateral consensus to address global problems. Exemptions for energy-intensive industries have been extensively adopted, but they largely impair environmental results.

Border tax adjustments should be analysed in depth as a feasible way out, bearing in mind that this solution seems to be easier to implement in the case of domestic environmental taxes rather than regulations. When considering energy products, the possibility of levying a compensatory duty on fuel imports clearly seems consistent with trade rules; however, problems could arise when a border tax adjustment is envisaged on

---

202 The 1992 proposal for a Directive introducing a carbon/energy tax was later revised. See COM(95) 172 final. In 1997, a new one – COM(97) 30 final – was put forward by the Commission revising the Community framework for taxing energy products. A further proposal was presented on 13 April 2011 (European Commission, 2011), but was withdrawn due to the Council's lack of support.

imports of goods that use an amount of carbon-intensive energy in their production process.

It must be recalled that a negative conclusion was reached on border tax adjustments in a GATT Report,[203] rejecting the principle of a *level playing field*, and suggesting that "…there is no difference between the competitive implications of the type raised by different environmental standards and the competitive consequences of many other policy differences between countries…". While this remark is generally correct as far as regulations are concerned, the possibility of border tax adjustments for environmental taxes levied on products, when these products are used as inputs in the production process of other products, was not rejected by a GATT Panel,[204] when the EC – together with Canada – challenged the *United States Superfund Amendments and Reauthorization Act* of 1986.

The *Superfund Act* authorised a program to clean up hazardous waste sites and deal with public health programmes caused by hazardous waste. It imposed a tax on certain chemicals with effect from 1 January 1987 and further levied a new tax on certain imported substances, entering into effect on 1 January 1989. The taxable imported substances were derivatives of chemicals subject to domestic tax on certain chemicals.

The amount of tax on any of the imported substances was equal in principle to the amount of tax which would have been imposed under the *Superfund Act* on the chemicals used as materials in the manufacture or production of the imported substance, if the taxable chemicals had been sold in the United States for use in the manufacture or production of the imported substances. Hence, the Panel concluded that, to the extent that the tax on certain imported substances was equivalent to the tax borne by like domestic substances as a result of the tax on certain chemicals, the tax met the national treatment requirement of Article III:2, first sentence, of the GATT.

The question of whether the ruling of the *Superfund* case could be applied when border tax adjustments are envisaged for products using a large amount of energy, not as a raw material, but as a combustion fuel consumed during the production process, must still be verified. In any case, it should be proven that the tax is levied on a product (the fuel utilised during the production process) and not on the process as such – to

---

203 GATT, *Dunkel Report on Trade and Environment*, 11 February 1992.

204 GATT, *United States Taxes on Petroleum and Certain Imported Substances (Superfund)*, Report of the Panel, 17 June 1987 (L6175 – 34S/136): "…To the extent that the tax on certain imported substances was equivalent to the tax borne by the like domestic substances as a result of the tax on certain chemicals, the tax met the national treatment requirement of Article III:2…".

avoid the ban of trade measures with extra-jurisdictional effects highlighted by the Tuna Panel Report.[205]

The *Superfund Act* envisaged the option to implement border tax adjustments if the chemicals subject to the domestic tax on certain chemicals constituted more than 50% of the weight or the value of the materials used to produce such imported substances – determined on the basis of the predominant method of production. According to this provision – uncontested in the Panel Report – it seems appropriate to levy a border tax adjustment even if the energy – that is taxed domestically – does not appear in a measurable physical quantity within the imported product, provided the value of energy represents a certain percentage of the total value of the imported commodity.

7. The relevant role of border tax adjustment as a complement to carbon pricing

Widespread support in public opinion for the protection of the environment, especially in the most industrialised – and largely polluted – countries, should not hide the risk that tough environmentally-friendly measures could be used as new, hidden, trade barriers. It is quite clear that there are fully legitimate reasons for applying different domestic environmental policies, which reflect local conditions, preferences and levels of development. Thus, when environmental measures concern domestic goods, the argument for using trade restrictions can only be protectionist in nature, and must be firmly rejected.

When, on the contrary, global environmental goods are at stake, the definition of international standards of environmental protection – as has been the case for technical, sanitary, and phytosanitary standards – seems to be an appropriate means to meet needs for environmental protection, while limiting negative impacts on trade. However, outside the technical framework, as a general rule, regulations do not represent the most cost-effective way to solve global environmental problems. There is currently a broad consensus that the most cost-effective instrument to address global warming is a worldwide energy/carbon tax with a uniform rate since, in this case, the reduction in carbon dioxide emissions will take place wherever the costs of such reductions are lower.

---

205 GATT, *United States – Restrictions on the Import of Tuna (Tuna Dolphin)*, Report of the Panel (DS29/R), 16 June 1994.

If this solution is not feasible in the short run, as some major countries cannot accept the same increase in energy taxation, unilateral initiatives are needed. However, in this case, new solutions – and border tax adjustments are probably the most effective – should be adopted to prevent the protection of the global commons from impairing competitive conditions for the most environmentally-friendly countries.

Hence, President Emmanuel Macron's suggestions in his speech at La Sorbonne appear quite significant. Macron has stressed the importance of ecological transition in shaping the new worldwide economic landscape and the crucial role that Europe could play by putting a price on carbon in curbing CO_2 emissions. He also remarked that, to be effective, the price put on carbon emissions could not be lower than €25-30 per tonne of CO_2. However, if a loss of competitiveness for European firms is to be avoided and the risk of carbon leakage prevented, border adjustments are needed, allowing products flowing from countries with no price on carbon to be taxed at the same rate levied on domestic production.

The discussion about new resources to be attributed to finance the European budget has finally started, and the need to introduce a levy on the use of fossil fuels emitting CO_2 is supported by the scientific community. But the political hurdles to be overcome are relevant, and the main one is the risk of a loss of external competitiveness for firms located in countries that unilaterally introduce a carbon price. A border tax adjustment is therefore an unavoidable complement of a CO_2 levy, if an effective policy of curbing CO_2 emissions and avoiding the risks of climate changes were put in place. Then, this remains as one of the cornerstones that is crucial in shaping the future Multiannual Financial Framework 2021-27.

CHAPTER 9

Conclusions

Considering the budgetary difficulties with which many euro area countries are confronted, that heavily limit options to engage in an effective policy promoting sustainable growth, monetary stability, social equilibrium and internal and external security, a decisive, multiple role must be played by Europe. Europe must strengthen democratic institutions – that are put in danger by the emerging nationalist attitude of many governments – with radical measures that reform existing Treaties and current policies, supporting growth while guaranteeing stability of the euro. The Union must also reduce, through employment-creating measures, the social tensions that are becoming unsustainable in many countries and, ultimately lower, through the automatic expansionary effects of GDP growth on tax receipts, constraints on national budgets. But the fiscal resources of the European budget are too limited. The way out of this deadlock is to be found in the political choice of supporting a project destined to the creation, by successive steps, of federal finance in the European Union, along a path similar to that taken to reach the final stage of the single currency. This draws from our developing awareness that the recent economic crisis was a sign: that it is unconceivable to proceed further in Europe with the previous kind of policies in the economic field and through *small steps* in the institutional area.

To start a radical change of the growth paradigm in Europe it is necessary to implement sustainable development in the economic, social and environmental fields. Accordingly, the main driver of this new model of growth should be public investments for producing not only material goods – that are desperately needed, like infrastructure (transport, energy, broadband) – but also non-material, in particular investments in basic research and higher education for supporting technological innovations, thus promoting an improvement in productivity and competitiveness of the European industry, that has now reached the technological frontier. But it is also necessary to support the production of European public goods in order to meet those needs of European citizens that are not satisfied by the market (environmental protection, the conservation of natural resources and cultural goods, personal services, mainly in favour of the most deprived people), and to realise the policy measures needed to guarantee external security – with an effective control of European borders and an aid policy supporting African countries, the principle origin of migratory flows – and internal security, endangered by terrorism. However, this increase in investments and, more generally, of public consumption, is limited by the limited size of the EU's budget, amounting to around 1% of GDP; this is totally insufficient to support the production of the public goods that are needed for achieving an in-depth transformation of the European economy.

Europe is confronted with a big challenge; to guarantee with certainty the future of the euro and the competitiveness of the European economy it is necessary to immediately start the building of a Fiscal Union endowed with a federal structure, assigning new own resources to the Union's budget, in particular putting a price on fossil fuels in proportion of their carbon content. In parallel, Europe must engage in an in-depth transformation of its economic structure, keeping pace with the dramatic wave of technological innovation, thus guaranteeing in the meantime the competitiveness of European production and a peaceful transition to less unequal social equilibrium, closer to full employment.

To face these challenges, it is quite clear that the limits of the Lisbon Treaty should be overcome and a process started that will be concluded, at the end of a transition period as was the case with the Monetary Union, by endowing the Commission with federal fiscal power. The task of the Commission, answerable to the European Parliament and the Council, the two branches of the legislative power, will be that of defining and implementing the general guidelines of European economic and fiscal policy and, at the same time, of guaranteeing an effective coordination of national choices. In the medium term, the Economic and Fiscal Union with a federal structure should be completed with the attribution of the power to rule foreign and security policy.

The time is ripe for this decisive choice; the crisis has laid bare the limits of national States, calls for a more efficient policy of support to sustainable development are increasing every day. But the only instrument at our disposal to promote European growth is represented by monetary policy, since the European Central Bank is the only federal institution in the economic field and, consequently, is the only one able to take decisions quickly and efficiently through a majority vote. Today, monetary policy, that has been able to overcome the crisis of sovereign debts and to drive back speculative attacks against the euro, has reached its limits and, confronting the risk of a new financial crisis, given the huge amount of liquidity flowing around the world, it is obliged to gradually cut down its expansionary policy in support of the European economy's growth.[206] Thus, if a new phase of sustainable development has to be opened, the use of fiscal instruments is unavoidable.

The Juncker Plan represents a significant step forward relatively to the previous trend, but it should be strengthened, giving the European budget new own resources, targeted at the management at the European level of a plan of sustainable development. In this framework a carbon tax – if complemented by border tax adjustments – could play a double role, endowing the European budget with adequate resources, while supporting the transition to a carbon-free model of growth. This could be the decisive step towards an effective Fiscal Union, that will be able to provide the investments needed to realise the technological leap forward that will guarantee the competitiveness of the European industry and the full employment of the workforce and, at the same time, the provision of the public goods European citizens are seeking. But further institutional changes are needed as well, that will bring about the creation of a European Treasury, which will represent, side by side with the European Central Bank, the second pillar of a federal power in the economic and monetary field.

---

206 The ECB has recently announced that at the end of 2018 the Quantitative Easing will be over, while the Federal Reserve has raised for the second time in this year the American rates. But the main question regards the sustainability, in an environment of increasing rates, of a global debt that amounts, according to recent estimates of the Institute of International Finance (*Global Debt Monitor*, April 2018), to around 237 trillion dollars.

References

M. Albertini, "La proposta del MFE per il dibattito sulla riforma istituzionale della Comunità", in *Il Federalista*, 1981, No. 2.

S. Ambec, M.A. Cohen, S. Elgie, P. Lanoie, *The Porter Hypothesis at 20: Can Environmental Regulation Enhance Innovation and Competitiveness?*, Resources for the Future Discussion Paper, 11/01, Washington, 2011.

N. Arnold, B. Barkbu, E. Ture, H. Wang, J. Yao, *A Central Fiscal Stabilization Capacity for the Euro Area*, IMF Staff Discussion Note, March 26, 2018.

A.B. Atkinson, *Inequality. What can be done?*, Harvard Univ. Press, 2015.

M.H. Babiker, "Climate change policy, market structure, and carbon leakage", in *Journal of International Economics*, March 2005.

A. Bénassi-Quéré *et al.*, *Reconciling risk-sharing with market discipline: A constructive approach to euro area reform*, CEPR Policy Insight, No. 91, January 2018.

M. Beblavý, G. Marconi, I. Maselli, *A European Unemployment Benefit Scheme. The rationale and the challenges ahead*, European Commission, Centre for European Policy Studies, Brussels 2015.

J. Bibow, *Making the Euro Viable: The Euro Treasury Plan*, Levy Institute WP, No. 84, July 2015.

O. Blanchard, F. Giavazzi, *Improving the SGP through a Proper Accounting of Public Investment*, CEPR Discussion Paper, No. 4220, 2004.

O. Blanchard, D. Leigh, *Growth Forecast Errors and Fiscal Multipliers*, IMF Working Paper 13/1, January 2013.

A.L. Bovenberg, "Green Tax Reforms and the Double Dividend: An Updated Reader's Guide", in *International Tax and Public Finance*, 1999, No. 6.

A.L. Bovenberg, L.H. Goulder, *Environmental Taxation and Regulation*, NBER Working Paper 8458, Cambridge MA, September 2001.

R. Castaldi, "La BCE: la forza di un'istituzione federale", Centro Studi sul Federalismo, Torino, Commento, No. 77, 14 marzo 2016.

J. Cimadomo, S. Hauptmeier, A.A. Palazzo, A. Popov, "Risk Sharing in the Euro Area", in *Economic Bulletin*, Issue 3, European Central Bank, 2018.

V. Constâncio, *Effectiveness of Monetary Union and the Capital Markets Union*, Speech at the Eurofil Conference, Malta, April 6, 2017.

G. Claeys, *New EMU stabilisation tool within the MFF will have minimal impact without deeper budget reform*, Brueghel Blog Post, May 9, 2018.

G. Claeys, *Are SBBS really the safe asset the euro area is looking for?*, Bruegel Blog Post, 28 May 2018.

G. Claeys, Z. Darvas, *The Commission's proposal for the next MFF: A glass half-full*, Bruegel Blog Post, 25 May 2018.

P. De Grauwe, *The Economics of Monetary Integration*, Oxford, Oxford University Press, 1997.

P. De Grauwe, "The Governance of a Fragile Eurozone", in *Australian Economic Review*, September 2012.

P. De Grauwe, *Macroeconomic Policies in the Eurozone since the Sovereign Debt Crisis*, Policy Paper No. 13, Euroforum KU Leuven, September 2014.

P. De Grauwe, Y. Ji, *The Legacy of Austerity in the Eurozone*, CEPS Commentary, 4 October 2014.

A. De Viti De Marco, *Principi di economia finanziaria*, Torino, Edizioni Scientifiche Einaudi, 1953.

J. Delbeke, *EU Energy Law*, Claeys & Casteels, Leuven, 2006.

S. Dullien, *A euro-area wide unemployment insurance as an automatic stabilizer: who benefits and who pays?*, Paper prepared for the European Commission, DG EMPL, Brussels, 2013.

B. Eichengreen, J. von Hagen, *Fiscal Restrictions and Monetary Union: Rationales, Repercussions, Reforms*, Saarbrucken, 2-3 October 1995.

European Commission, *Report of the Study Group on the Role of Public Finance in European Integration (MacDougall Report)*, Brussels, 1977.

European Commission, *Proposal for a Council Directive introducing a tax on carbon dioxide emissions and energy*, COM(92) 226 final, Brussels, 30 June 1992.

European Commission, *Growth, Competitiveness, Employment. The Challenges and Ways Forward into the 21st Century*, White Paper, COM(93) 700, Brussels, 5 December 1993.

European Commission, "Stable Money, Sound Finances. Community Public Finance in the Perspective of EMU", in *European Economy*, Brussels, 1993, No. 53.

European Commission, *Towards a stability pact*, Note for the Monetary Committee, Brussels, 10 January 1996.

European Commission, *A stability pact to ensure budgetary discipline*, Note for the Monetary Committee, Brussels, 18 March 1996.

European Commission, *Ensuring budgetary discipline in stage three of Emu*, Note for the Monetary Committee, Brussels, 19 July 1996.

European Commission, *Smarter energy taxation for the EU: proposal for a revision of the Energy Taxation Directive*, COM(2011) 168/3, Brussels, 2011.

European Commission, *Proposal for a Council Directive amending Directive 2003/96/EC restructuring the Community framework for the taxation of energy products and electricity*, COM(2011) 169 final, Brussels, 13 April 2011.

European Commission, *Six-pack? Two-pack? Fiscal compact? A short guide to the new EU fiscal governance*, Brussels, 2012.

European Commission, *A blueprint for a deep and genuine Economic and Monetary Union. Launching a European debate*, COM(2012) 777 final, Brussels, 28 November 2012.

European Commission, *Making the best use of the flexibility within the existing rules of the stability and growth pact*, COM(2015) 012 final, Brussels, 10 February 2015.

European Commission, *Revenue for EMU: A contribution to the debate on Fiscal Union*, Taxation Papers, WP No. 54, Brussels, 2015.

European Commission, *Shared Vision, Common Action: A Stronger Europe. A Global Strategy for the European Union's Foreign and Security Policy*, Brussels, June 2016.

European Commission, *Strengthening European Investments for jobs and growth: Towards a second phase of the European Fund for Strategic Investments and a new European External Investment Plan*, COM(2016) 581 final, Brussels, 14 September 2016.

European Commission, *Building a fair, competitive and stable corporate tax system for the EU*, COM(2016) 682 final, Strasbourg, 25 October 2016.

European Commission, *White Paper on the Future of Europe. Reflections and Scenarios for the EU27 by 2025*, COM(2017) 2015, Brussels, 1 March 2017.

European Commission, *Reflection Paper on the Deepening of the Economic and Monetary Union*, COM(2017) 291, Brussels, 31 May 2017.

European Commission, *A Global Strategy for the European Union*, 19 June 2017.

European Commission, *Reflection Paper on the Future of EU Finances*, Brussels, 28 June 2017.

European Commission, *Further Steps towards Completing Europe's Economic and Monetary Union: a Roadmap*, COM(2017) 821 final, Brussels, 6 December 2017.

European Commission, *A European Minister of Economy and Finance*, COM(2017) 823 final, Brussels, 6 December 2017.

European Commission, *Proposal for a Council Directive laying down provisions for strengthening fiscal responsibility and the medium-term budgetary orientation in the Member States*, COM(2017) 824 final, 6 December 2017.

European Commission, *Proposal for a Council Directive laying down rules relating to the corporate taxation of a significant digital presence*, COM(2018) 147 final, Brussels, 21 March 2018.

European Commission, *Proposal for a Council Directive on the common system of a digital services tax on revenues resulting from the provision of certain digital services*, COM(2018) 148 final, Brussels, 21 March 2018.

European Commission, *A Modern Budget for a Union that Protects, Empowers and Defends. The Multiannual Financial Framework for 2021-2027*, COM(2018) 321 final, Brussels, 2 May 2018.

European Fiscal Board, *Assessment of the prospective fiscal stance appropriate for the euro area*, Brussels, 20 June 2017.

European Parliament, *Draft Report on reform of the European Union's system of own resources*, 2017 /2053(INI), Rapporteurs G. Deprez, J. Lewandowski, Brussels, 10 January 2018.

European Systemic Risk Board, *ESBies; Safety in tranches*, ESRB, Working Paper Series, No. 21, September 2016.

Eurostat, *Which sector is the main employer in the EU Member States?* 24 October 2017.

F. Fabbrini, *The fiscal compact, the "Golden Rule", and the paradox of European federalism*, Tilburg Law School Legal Studies Research Paper Series, No. 013/2013.

O. Fontana, "Investire nelle strutture sociali dell'UE: passare dai principi all'azione", Centro Studi sul Federalismo, Commento, No. 125, Torino, 5 febbraio 2018.

O. Fontana, *The Debate on Eurozone Fiscal Capacity*, Centro Studi sul Federalismo, Policy Paper No. 35, Torino, July 2018.

O. Fontana, S. Vannuccini, *Conventional Direction to Unconventional Measures: Using Quantitative Easing to Shape Eurozone Fiscal Capacity*, Centro Studi sul Federalismo Research Paper, Turin, May 2016.

L. Fransen, G. del Bufalo, E. Reviglio, *Boosting Investments in social infrastructure in Europe*, Report of the High-level Task Force on investing in Social Infrastructure in Europe chaired by R. Prodi and C. Sautter, Discussion Paper 074, Brussels, 23 January 2018.

Future Financing of the EU, Final Report and Recommendations of the High Level Group on Own Resources (Mario Monti Chairman), Brussels, December 2016.

GATT Working Party Report, *Border Tax Adjustment*, L3464, 2 December 1970.

F. Giavazzi, M. Pagano, *Non-keynesian effects of fiscal policy changes: international evidence and the Swedish experience*, NBER WP 5332, National Bureau of Economic Research, November 1995.

L.H. Goulder, "Environmental Taxation and the 'Double Dividend': A Reader's Guide", in *International Tax and Public Finance*, 1995, 2, 2.

D. Gros, C. Egenhofer, *Climate Change and Trade. Taxing carbon at the border?*, Brussels, CEPS – Centre for European Policy Studies, 2010.

D.R. Helm, R. Smale, J. Philipps, *Too Good to Be True? The UK's Climate Change Record*, Oxford, New College, 10 December 2007.

J. Hillman, *Changing Climate for Carbon Taxes. Who's Afraid of the WTO?* The German Marshall Fund of the United States, Climate and Energy Paper Series, Washington, July 2013.

A. Iozzo, S. Micossi, M.T. Salvemini, *A new budget for the European Union?* CEPS Policy Brief, No. 159, May 2008.

A. Iozzo, *Aspetti istituzionali della procedura di adozione del Multiannual Financial Framework: un nuovo contesto per il 2021-2025*, Centro Studi sul Federalismo, Torino, 2018.

J.C. Juncker, *State of the Union's Address 2017*, Brussels, 13 September 2017.

K. Kosonen, "Regressivity of environmental taxation: myth or reality?", in J.E. Milne, M.S. Andersen (eds.), *Handook of Research on Environmental Taxation*, Edward Elgar, 2012.

C. Lagarde, *A Compass to Prosperity: The Next Steps of Euro Area Economic Integration*, German Institute for Economic Research, Berlin, 26 March 2018.

P. Low, G. Marceau, J. Reinaud, *The Interface between the Trade and Climate Change Regimes: Scoping the Issues*, WTO, Staff Working Paper ERSD-2011-1.

"Il Memorandum Monnet del 3 maggio 1950", in M. Albertini, *Il federalismo. Antologia e definizioni*, Il Mulino, Bologna, 1979.

Initiative pour l'Europe. Discours d'Emmanuel Macron: *Pour une Europe souveraine, unie, démocratique*, Paris, 26 Septembre 2017.

IMF, *Revisiting the Economic Case for Fiscal Union in the Euro Area*, IMF Departmental Paper, Washington, February 2018.

Italian Position Paper, *Reforming the European Monetary Union in a stronger European Union*, Rome, 13 December 2017.

Italian Non-Paper, *Migration Compact. Contribution to an EU-Strategy for External Action on Migration*, Presidenza del Consiglio, Roma, 15 April 2016.

A. Italianer, M. Vanheukelen, "Proposals for Community Stabilization Mechanisms: Some Historical Applications", in *European Economy: Reports and Studies*, 1993, No. 5.

A.M. MacDonald, H.C. Bonsor, B.E. Ó Dochartaig, R.G. Taylor, "Quantitative Maps of Groundwater Resources in Africa", in *Environmental Resource Letters*, 2012, 7.

A. Majocchi, "Le federalism fiscal et la function redistributive: le cas de la Communauté Européenne", in *Revue française de finances publiques*, 1987, No. 20.

A. Majocchi, M. Rey, "A Special Financial Support Scheme in Economic and Monetary Union: Need and Nature, in The Economics of Community Public Finance", in *European Economy: Reports and Studies*, 1993, No. 5.

A. Majocchi, "The Rationale behind Energy Taxation. The European Commission's Proposal of an Energy-Carbon Tax", in IFA, *Environmental Taxes and Charges*, Florence, 1993.

A. Majocchi, "Carbon-energy tax, emission permits and border tax adjustments", in L. Kreiser (ed.), *Carbon Pricing, Growth and the Environment*, Edwar Elgar, 2012.

A. Majocchi, "Politica fiscale e principio di sussidiarietà nell'Unione europea", in E. Giardina, F. Osculati, M. Rey, *Federalismo*, Franco Angeli, Milano, 1996.

A. Majocchi, *A European Fund for Growth and Employment: A First Step Toward a Eurozone Budget*, German Marshall Fund Policy Brief, June 2014.

A. Majocchi, *Un piano per l'Europa. Sviluppo sostenibile e occupazione*, Bologna, Il Mulino, 2015.

A. Majocchi, "Migration Compact and African Growth", Centro Studi sul Federalismo, Comment, No. 92, Turin, 7 November 2016.

A. Majocchi, *Progressivity in Financing EU Budget*, Centro Studi sul Federalismo, Policy Paper No. 22, Torino, January 2017.

M. Messori, S. Micossi, *Counterproductive Proposals on Euro Area Reform by French and German Economists*, CEPS Policy Insights, No. 2018/04, February 2018.

W. Moesen, P. van Rompuy, *The Growth of Government Size and Fiscal Decentralization*, Paper prepared for Iipf Congress, Brussels, 1990.

D. Moro, *For a federal European Unemployment Insurance Scheme*, U.E.F. Reflection Paper, Brussels, March 2016.

R.A. Musgrave, "The nature of Budgetary Balance and the Case for a Capital Budget", in *American Economic Review*, 1939 .

R.A. Musgrave, *The Theory of Public Finance. A Study in Public Economy*, New York, McGraw-Hill, 1959.

W.E. Oates, *Fiscal Federalism*, Harcourt Brace Jovanovich, 1972.

M.V. Pauly, "Income redistribution as a Local Public Good", in *Journal of Public Economics*, 1973, Vol. 2, No. 1.

G. Peters, E. Hertwich, "CO_2 Embodied in International Trade with Implications for Global Climate Policy", in *Environmental Science and Technology*, 2008.

T. Piketty, *Capital in the Twenty-First Century*, Harvard Univ. Press, 2014.

J. Pisani-Ferry, J. Zettelmeyer, *Messori and Micossi's reading of the Franco-German 7+7 paper is a misrepresentation*, CEPS Commentary, 19 February 2018.

J. Pisani-Ferry J., A. Italianer, R. Lescure, "Stabilization Properties of Budgetary Systems: A Simulation Analysis", in *European Economy: Reports and Studies*, 1993, No. 5.

K. Palmer, W.E. Oates, P.R. Portney, "Tightening Environmental Standards: The Benefit-Cost or the No-Cost Paradigm?", in *Journal of Economic Perspectives*, 1995, 9, 4.

M.E. Porter, *The Competitive Advantage of Nations*, New York, Free Press, 1990.

M.E. Porter, C. Van der Linde, "Toward a New Conception of the Environment-Competitiveness Relationship", in *Journal of Economic Perspectives*, 1995, 9, 4.

R. Repasi, *Legal options for an additional EMU fiscal capacity*, European Parliament, Policy department C, Brussels, 2013.

F. Rossollillo, *Città, territorio, istituzioni nella società post-industriale*, Napoli, Guida editori, 1983.

E. Rubio, D. Rinaldi, T. Pellerin-Carlin, *Investment in Europe: making the best of the Juncker Plan. With case studies on digital infrastructure and energy efficiency*, Notre Europe Studies and Report, No. 109, March 2016.

W. Schäuble, *Non-paper for paving the way towards a Stability Union*, mimeo, 2017.

A. Spinelli, *PCI, che fare? Riflessioni su strategia e obiettivi della sinistra*, Torino, Einaudi, 1978.

J.E. Stiglitz, *The price of inequality. How today's divided society endangers our future*, New York, W.W. Norton, 2012.

J.E. Stiglitz, N. Stern, *Report of the High-Level Commission on Carbon Prices*, World Bank, Washington D.C., 2017.

The Five Presidents' Report: Completing Europe's Economic and Monetary Union, Brussels, 22 June 2015.

G.R. Timilsina, *Where is the carbon tax after thirty years of research?*, Policy Research working paper; No. WPS 8493. Washington, D.C.: World Bank Group, June 2018.

T.R. Tørsløv, L.S. Wier, G. Zucman, *The Missing Profits of Nations*, NBER Working Paper No. 24701, June 2018.

Towards a genuine Economic and Monetary Union, Report by the President of the European Council, Brussels, 5 December 2012.

R.W. Tresch, *Public Finance. A Normative Approach*, Business Publications Inc., Plano, 1981.

A. Watt, *Quantitative easing with bite: a proposal for conditional overt monetary financing of public investment*, IMK WP 148, March 2015.

J. Weidman, F. Villeroy de Galhau, *L'Europe à la croisée des chemins*, Banque de France, February 2016.

M.L. Weitzman, "Prices vs. Quantities", in *The Review of Economic Studies*, October 1974.

G. Wolff, *A budget for Europe's monetary union*, Bruegel Policy Contribution No. 22, Brussels, 2012.

Webliography

https://library.harvard.edu/sites/default/files/1947_marshall.pdf (Original text of Marshall speech).

www.epa.gov/ghgemissions/global-greenhouse-gas-emissions-data.

www.globalcarbonatlas.org/en/CO2-emissions.

Federalism

The book series Federalism, run by the Centro Studi sul Federalismo/ Centre for Studies on Federalism (CSF) aims to disseminate knowledge in the field of studies on federalism, as well as to feed the academic and public debate and support the activity of decision-makers, confronted with demands for autonomy by local governments, along with forms of regional and world integration needed to govern global processes.

The book series is divided into two sub-series: Studies and Classics. The former mostly contains the research outcome and the proceedings of conferences and seminars promoted by the Centre, while the latter consists in reprints of the federalist classic works and English translations of Italian federalists' works.

The CSF is a think tank that carries out activities of interdisciplinary research, documentation, information regarding domestic and supranational federalism, developments in the area of regional and continental integration – first and foremost the European Union – and problems related to the world order and the process of democratisation of the international system. The CSF has been founded under the auspices of the Compagnia di San Paolo and the Universities of Turin, Pavia and Milan.

Centro Studi sul Federalismo
Piazza Vincenzo Arbarello 8
10122 Torino – Italy
Tel. + 39 011.6705024 Fax + 39 011.6705081
E-mail: info@csfederalismo.it
Website: www.csfederalismo.it

Editorial Board

Series titles

No.1 – Giovanni Finizio and Ernesto Gallo (eds.), *Democracy at the United Nations. UN Reform in the Age of Globalisation*, 2012.

No.2 – Roberto Castaldi (ed.), *Immanuel Kant and Alexander Hamilton, the Founders of Federalism. A Political Theory for Our Time*, 2013.

No.3 – Claudio Giulio Anta (ed.), *Lord Lothian: The Paths of Federalism. Writings and Speeches*, 2014.

No.4 – Filippo Maria Giordano and Stefano dell'Acqua (eds.), *"Die Welt war meine Gemeinde". Willem A. Visser 't Hoof – A Theologian for Europe between Ecumenism and Federalism*, 2014.

No.5 – Giampiero Bordino (ed.), *A New Right for Democracy and Development in Europe. The European Citizens' Initiative (ECI)*, 2015.

No.6 – Filippo Maria Giordano, *Unity through Diversity. An Insight into Federalism and Ecumenism within Italian Protestantism*, 2016.

No.7 – Lucio Levi, Giampiero Bordino and Antonio Mosconi (eds.), *Federalism. A Political Theory for Our Time*, 2016.

No.8 – Lorenzo Vai, Pier Domenico Tortola and Nicoletta Pirozzi (eds.), *Governing Europe. How to Make the EU More Efficient and Democratic*, 2017.

No.9 – Korwa G. Adar, Giovanni Finizio and Angela Meyer (eds.), *Building Regionalism from Below. The Role of Parliaments and Civil Society in Regional Integration in Africa*, 2017.

No.10 – Alberto Majocchi, *European budget and sustainable growth. The Role of a Carbon Tax*, 2018.

www.peterlang.com

FSC
www.fsc.org
MIX
Papier | Fördert gute Waldnutzung
FSC® C083411

Kolibri 360 GmbH
Ferdinand-Jühlke-Straße 7
99095 Erfurt, Deutschland
produktsicherheit@kolibri360.de